LATER, GATOR

LAURENCE YEP

 HOUGHTON MIFFLIN   BOSTON • MORRIS PLAINS, NJ

California • Colorado • Georgia • Illinois • New Jersey • Texas

To my real Oscar, gone but not forgotten,
And to my patient brother, Spike.
—L. Y.

Later, Gator, by Laurence Yep. Copyright © 1995 by Laurence Yep.
Reprinted by arrangement with Hyperion Books for Children.

Houghton Mifflin Edition, 2001

Printed in the U. S. A.

ISBN: 0-618-06279-3

3456789-B-06 05 04 03 02

Later, Gator

LAURENCE YEP

chapter one

The alligator was Mother's fault. She told me to buy
something special. Mother, as usual, blames me. She
says that I've got more imagination than brains.

That's not my little brother's problem. Last Christmas I gave him a pair of socks. Bobby was too dumb to
understand the insult. Instead of getting mad, he said
to me, "They're neat-o and just what I wanted."

Yeah, sure, I thought to myself.

Bobby had to put on his new socks right away and
wriggle his toes at me. "They're very warm and comfortable. Thank you," he said.

Do you see what I mean? Bobby is a walking Hall-
mark card.

Mother had understood, though. So this year, on
Friday, the day before Bobby's eighth birthday, she
took me aside. "Why can't you get along with your little
brother? What has he ever done to you?"

"Nothing," I confessed. That was the trouble. What

kind of little brother doesn't bug his big brother? Bobby was not normal.

Mother clicked her tongue. "Everybody else likes your brother. He's so sweet."

"Bobby's a regular mint chocolate bar, all right," I said, and thought to myself, And I am a raisin cookie.

"Then why haven't you ever bought him something special?" Mother demanded. She would make a good prosecutor.

"You always said it's the spirit that counts," I grumbled.

Mother frowned. "Only a mean person buys a cheap pair of white cotton socks."

"He liked the baseball."

Mother folded her hands in front of her. "Which you then used and lost."

"The Christmas before I got him comic books," I pointed out.

"Which he couldn't read."

"I read them to him," I said. Mother just looked at me until I admitted, "Sometimes."

"You treat him like he's an enemy. Don't you love your brother?" Mother asked.

"Of course I do," I lied. (But really, how can I love a little angel who makes me feel mean and selfish and bad?)

"Then show your love," Mother said. "Get something Bobby wants."

I tried to weasel out of it. "I can't afford the official Willie Mays baseball glove."

"No, I mean something he wants even more. I've talked it over with your father, and he's agreed that Bobby is now old enough to have a pet," Mother said.

She went to a cabinet and took out a big paper bag. From the bag, she slid out a kidney-shaped plastic tray. A wall of transparent plastic some three inches high ran around the edge of the tray. Part of the bottom rose up into an island in the center. A plastic palm tree grew from the island's middle.

"I got the idea when he was watching a nature show on TV. He likes animals," Mother said. "He always wants to go to the zoo or the Academy of Sciences." The academy was in Golden Gate Park and had an aquarium, a hall with stuffed animals, and a reptile section.

It wasn't fair, I told myself. I figured he watched educational shows to please our parents and to make me look bad. I'll take the Three Stooges over a nature show anytime.

"Then I saw an ad in the newspaper," Mother said, "and I bought this. It's a turtle home. You go down to the department store. They've got turtles on sale. You can buy him a pet."

Feeling miserable but caught, I promised.

For the rest of the week, I put it off. There was no

fun in giving Bobby something he wanted. Instead, I just hung around the apartment and moped.

On the morning of his birthday, he was up bright and early and jumping around, pretending to catch fly balls over the shoulder like Willie Mays. He had made so much noise that I had got up early, too, even though it was Saturday.

Mother served his favorite breakfast. We each had a scrambled egg with rice and slices of Chinese sausage. The problem was that Mother served it every morning. It was typical of Bobby to play up to Mother that way. I would have asked for scrambled eggs, bacon, and toast.

When Father asked Bobby what he wanted to do on his birthday, Bobby volunteered to help him in the fish shop. Any normal kid would have asked for money for a movie—for him and for his older brother. Boy, he really drove me crazy.

After Father and Bobby left for work, Mother stood over me. "Well, did you buy Bobby's pet?" she asked.

I squirmed on my chair. "I didn't want to get it too soon. If Bobby found it, it would ruin the surprise."

"I thought so." Mother handed me a folded-up piece of paper. "I cut out the ad from the newspaper so you would know where to go. After you wash the dishes, go down and buy Bobby's pet."

"That's Bobby's chore today," I whined.

"It's his birthday," Mother said. "I have to buy tonight's dinner. When I come home, I want to find that turtle waiting for me. You can leave it in our bedroom until we give out the presents." She wasn't going to leave me any way to escape. "If you need money, go down to the garbage cans. I saw lots of empty soda bottles."

chapter two

After Mother left, I heaved a big sigh. Going into the kitchen, I turned on the radio for music and began washing the dishes.

As I was finishing up, I saw the newspaper ad on the table. It was for a department store in the Stonestown mall, where Mother worked. It would take me most of the morning to get out there.

Above the address was a big drawing of a boy and girl gazing happily at a turtle. It was grinning back from a plastic bowl like the one Mother had bought. In big type, the ad announced the turtles were on sale for fifty cents. Then I saw the small print: BABY ALLIGATORS ON SALE. And like an omen, the radio began playing a funny song from the past. "See you later, alligator," the radio sang. "After a while, crocodile."

If there had been a lightbulb over my head, it would have suddenly shone as bright as the sun. Carefully I reviewed Mother's words. As far as I could remember, she had said to buy Bobby a pet. I chuckled. Poor Mother. She thought she had trapped me, but she had given me a loophole.

A plan began to build in my mind. First, though, I called up the department store having the sale. When I got the operator, I asked her, "I'd like to buy my brother something special from your pet department. If he doesn't like it, can I return it?"

"You can return anything within seventy-two hours after the sale." She added, "But the pet has to be alive."

"It won't be here long enough to die," I laughed, and hung up. I imagined what would happen tonight when Bobby opened his present. He would probably run shrieking from the room.

In my mind, I played out many marvelous scenes, ranging from a horrified Bobby to an outraged one. In any case, I would have to return it and get my money back. At the same time Mother would learn her lesson, too.

It was the perfect gift. I could keep my promise to Mother because it would be nature stuff as well as something special. I could keep my promise to myself because it would be weird enough.

The only trouble was the price. I went to my bureau drawer and counted the change in the old cup. Then I went to my secret treasure vault, which was a copy of *Tom Swift, Junior.* Between pages 42 and 43, I kept a *ly-cee* from our Uncle Tim and Aunt Norma. A ly-cee is a small red envelope.

I slipped out the little bright red envelope and took out the money folded in there. I searched for the other envelope from Uncle Curtis and Aunt Ethel. Too late, I realized I had spent it on snacks last month when I had seen a movie. Still, I had other reserves. Getting down on all fours, I hunted under my bed and found some spare change. In the kitchen I found some empty soda bottles.

Then I went to the garbage cans. More empty soda bottles were there, just as Mama had said. With all the returns, I had just enough money to get Bobby his special surprise. I could hardly wait.

At this point, I ought to explain my philosophy of life. Older brothers are put on this earth to help prepare younger brothers for reality. Parents pick on the first child. I think they call it "building character." However, they spend so much energy building the first child's character that they're worn out by the time the second one comes along. So the first child has to take up the slack or the second child won't have any character at all. In fact, an older brother owes it to his little brother to pick on him. We do it out of love because we want our little brothers to grow up to be more than jellyfish.

It took a cable car and two buses to get out to the Stonestown shopping mall. It had been sunny in Chinatown, but in that neighborhood a cloud hid the sun.

The store itself was a three-story brick box occupying one corner of the mall. By the escalator was a directory to the store. I had to go up three flights to the very top, where there was a tremendous racket. I just followed the sound of barking to the pet station. I didn't see how the clerk could stand it.

He was a plump man whose gray jacket barely buttoned in front. When he saw me, he leaned against a counter so that his big belly strained his jacket even more. He made a big show of examining me. When I opened my mouth to speak, he put up his hand. "Uh-uh. Don't say a word. I've got to study you for a while longer. This is all very scientific. Match the right pet with the right person, and you've got two happy critters."

"I'd like an alligator please," I said firmly.

He was so surprised he popped a button. He ignored the wooden disk as it flew through the air. "But," he protested, "you're a hamster man if I ever saw one. I'll give you a good deal."

I was usually a sucker for a bargain, but a hamster was . . . well, cute. I couldn't see the point in giving Bobby something he'd like. "No thanks. I came to get an alligator."

The clerk made a loud buzzing sound like on the quiz shows when someone misses an answer. "Wrong, wrong, wrong! That's why a civilian should never be allowed to pick his own pet. An alligator's a terrible choice for you. You need warmth. You need cute. You need cuddly."

I retrieved the button and handed it to him. "It's not for me. It's for my brother," I explained.

Irritated, he tapped the button on the glass top of the counter. "You should have brought him along then. If I can't observe him, how can I tell if his little friend should be feathered, furred, or finned?"

Who knew Bobby better than me? "He needs an alligator," I insisted.

"Tell me about your brother," he suggested as he pocketed the button.

"I would like an alligator," I repeated.

"If it has to be a reptile, how about a cute turtle?" He stepped aside. There, in a huge tank, were the turtles Mother had wanted me to buy. They were tiny things, only about three inches long. They almost completely covered a rock in the center of the tank. Layer after layer, they rose in an ever-changing, ever-squirming pyramid. Still others formed a green mosaic in the water. Just beyond them was a table filled with plastic turtle homes like the one Mother had bought.

"I'll even throw in a nickname for it," he offered.

From his back pocket, he took out a list. "I have here a compendium of the hundred most popular pet names. Every one is a surefire winner."

"No, I'd like an alligator," I persisted.

He raised one eyebrow as he put away his list. Then he led me to another tank. There were three alligators, each about eight inches long from snout to tail tip.

Baby alligators were something only . . . well . . . a mother alligator could love. They looked like green sticks, dark on top and yellow on the bottom. Their little legs dangled beneath them as they floated quietly. Their heads seemed to be mostly mouth, and their eyes stuck up like two little marbles moving above the surface. Even so, their teeth looked as fine and sharp as ivory needles.

"They're nothing but floating appetites. You really think your brother deserves one?" he asked.

Staring at their needle-sharp teeth, I hesitated. "I don't know."

He winked. "I'll give you a good deal on a goldfish?"

Bobby would have bought a goldfish. They were harmless. Just like Bobby. However, goldfish and hamsters would not develop Bobby's character at all.

"No," I said. "I want an alligator." I crouched, studying the leathery creatures. "In fact, I want that one." I pointed to the one drifting in the middle.

When the clerk bent over to look, the front flaps of

his jacket hung down. "What's so special about that one?"

"It's got the longest teeth," I said. "See?"

The clerk looked across the tank at me. "Son, I can see I've underestimated you considerably. You're not a hamster man. You're skunk, pure and simple."

chapter three

I could see the bus was packed before it even pulled up to the curb. When it opened its doors, I saw that people were even standing on the steps. I faced a solid wall of elbows and briefcases and bags.

The other people behind me gave up. They turned away to wait for the next bus. However, I treated it like a football game. Holding my package tight against my stomach, I lowered my head and squeezed under the elbows. When a briefcase banged me, I shrugged it off like a tackler.

As the door sighed shut, a man glared down at me. "Watch it, sonny."

I pretended to ignore him, but I could feel his knee in my side. Still cradling the alligator's box against me, I thrust my bus ticket through the forest of legs. From the other side, I heard the driver's puncher click. Wriggling my arm back, I stowed my bus ticket in my pocket just as the bus gave a lurch.

I fell against the man. "Sorry," I muttered.

He gave me a sour look. "Couldn't you wait for the next bus?"

When the bus pulled out into traffic, the alligator got excited. As it began to move from side to side, it shifted its weight around inside the box. The movement made the box hard to balance. Hurriedly I clutched it in both arms so I wouldn't drop it.

At the department store, the clerk had poked holes in the box so the alligator could breathe. It also made it easier to hear the alligator.

Slither, slither, slither.

When the bus jerked with a halt at a stoplight, I fell against the man again. "Sorry," I mumbled a second time.

I expected another snide remark, but the man only stared at the box.

"Just what have you got in there, sonny?" he asked.

I got to my feet and tried to brace myself for the bus's jerky motion. "It's an alligator," I said.

The bus driver must have overheard me on the other side of the wall of people. "Hey, you can't bring an alligator on board."

I wasn't about to walk all the way to Chinatown with an alligator. "It's small and it's safely boxed," I argued. "Show me a sign that says I can't have it."

"Well, I say so, kid," the bus driver snapped.

"That's not good enough. My uncle Curtis says that

if it isn't posted in writing, it's not legal. And he's a lawyer." I added helpfully, "He sues people."

"Okay, kid," the driver sighed. "Just don't point that thing at me."

"When it's inside the box, it's hard to tell which end is which," I said to apologize.

Suddenly people got real edgy around me. They began pulling back, so I actually had room to spread my legs.

At the next stop, the man and the other people around me hurried off. At the time, I was too grateful to think it was odd. Instead, I climbed up the steps and joined the mob packed inside the bus itself.

Slither, slither, slither.

"Shh!" I said to the alligator.

That only made the alligator thrash around angrily. It might be small, but it was already very strong.

Slither, slither, slither.

As I struggled to hold the box, people were staring at me curiously. When the alligator thumped its tail against the cardboard sides, people became nervous.

It was funny how many of them got off at the next stop. As my bus roared away, they didn't leave. Instead, they milled around as if waiting for another bus.

I spread my legs for better balance and gripped a railing. I tried to rest the box against my hip. However, when the alligator bounced off one side, I almost lost it altogether. In front of me was a man in a leather jacket. He shot up out of his seat and edged around me. "Here, kid," he said. Stumbling, he lurched through the crowded bus to the rear doors.

Standing beside me was an elderly lady. A bright blue bandanna was wrapped tightly around her head. I smiled at her. "Would you like the seat?"

At that moment, the alligator thrashed around and the box jerked up from my hip. Behind her glasses, the lady's eyes got very wide. Turning away from me, she said, "Excuse me." Wriggling, she followed the other man to the back of the bus.

There was a woman on the other seat of the bench. She eyed me anxiously. When I started to sit down, she said, "Wait a moment."

She got up and slid through the crowd. I plopped down on the bench and slid over into the seat by the window. No one else sat down. Instead, everyone around me began to whisper and point at me.

Setting the box on my lap, I held it with both hands. I was careful, though, not to cover up the airholes.

I had to transfer two more times—once to a bus and once to a cable car. Each time, I had no trouble getting a seat, though it was crowded. By the time I got to Chinatown, I had begun to fantasize. Was it me, or was it the alligator? Maybe it was both.

Anyway you cut it, I didn't care.

chapter four

We lived in a three-story apartment on Clay Street just to the east of Mason Street. A mattress sagged against one yellow wall of the hallway of our apartment house. I had expected it to be hauled away each month, but each month it stayed, sagging a bit more against the wall.

I took the steps two at a time. The metal buffers on the edges of the steps clicked musically under my shoes. If I climbed in a certain rhythm, the stairs made a kind of music. I could pretend I was a dancer.

At the second landing, I could hear Mrs. Lee's Chinese opera. I only like the fighting tunes. Sometimes, though, when I was with Mama and a love song came on, tears would come to her eyes. Hurriedly she'd open her big black purse with a loud snap. When I'd ask her why she was crying, she would just wave her Kleenex. "You need more Chinese school," she would say.

Maybe my Chinese wasn't good enough. But Mama and Papa also used that excuse when they didn't want to explain something.

On the third landing, I wrinkled my nose. Mr. Wong, our landlord, was boiling another of his herbal cures. From behind his door, I could hear him coughing. He'd had the cough all my life, and all my life he'd been going to herbalists to get medicines. Each of them smelled worse than the last.

Mama kept a can of pine scent by the doorway because of Mr. Wong. Anytime he boiled up one of his cures, she would spray the pine scent along the bottom of the door. The scent was supposed to provide an invisible barrier against the stink. It never did.

I took a deep breath and covered the breathing holes of the box. Then I ran the last steps to our door. When I lifted my hand away to get my key, the alligator started slithering inside the box. Mr. Wong's medicine really seemed to upset it because it bounced from one side to the other. The weight kept shifting so violently that I almost dropped the box.

Somehow I managed to keep hold of it as I slid through the door. Slamming it behind me, I set the box on the floor. "Mother?" I called out.

She wasn't home. For her sake, I sprayed the pine scent along the door. Then I turned back to the box.

Slither, slither, slither.

"Bobby?" I shouted. The goody-goody still hadn't come back.

Kneeling, I undid the string and lifted the lid of the box.

The alligator hadn't looked nearly so big in the department store.

It hadn't looked so frisky either. It just seemed to surge up out of the box. I barely clapped the lid down in time. For a moment, I could feel its snout shoving at the cardboard. Then I was able to force the lid back on top of the box. As I held the lid down, I began to think of all the questions I should have asked the department store clerk.

Can alligators bite through cardboard lids? Do alligators get mad? How big do they grow? Do they hold grudges?

Thoughts like these raced through my mind as I tried to keep the alligator from escaping. When it finally subsided, I didn't dare lift my hands. As I knelt there, another question came to me: How do I wrap it?

I might still have been sitting there if Mama and Bobby hadn't finally come home. "Oh, that Mr. Wong," Mama said. "Ugh. Don't breathe, Bobby."

Mother had probably stopped by Father's fish shop to pick up some shrimp for tonight. It would be like Bobby to leave the fish shop and help her with her packages.

I heard her key fumble at the door. "It's not locked," she said in surprise, and turned the doorknob.

The smell of Mr. Wong's medicine blew heavily into the apartment. Mama stared down at me, her key still in her hand. "Teddy, what are you doing there?"

The stench of the herbal cure roused the alligator once again. Something thumped against the lid, and I sat back, startled. "Watch out!"

The lid bobbed up and down under more blows.

"What's that?" Bobby asked. He set down his shopping bags as the lid finally got knocked ajar.

"Run!" I shouted as a thin green tail waved in the air.

With the ignorance of youth, Bobby simply lifted the lid up. "It's an alligator!" he cried in delight.

I was going to make up for my crime by throwing myself between Bobby and the alligator. However, the alligator merely poked its snout out of the box.

Bobby stared down at it. "Wow, that's neat-neat-neat-o!"

Mama had finally found her voice. "Whose alligator is that?" I think she was hoping that I was only alligator-sitting for someone else.

I didn't dare look up at her as I confessed, "It's Bobby's." I added, "I bought it as a special birthday present."

"You did?" Bobby's face lit up. "This is the neatest present anyone's ever given me."

I stared at him dumbly. "You want it?"

"Of course." He looked down almost warmly. "I always wanted a pet."

"It's an alligator," Mother said.

"It's just like the ones in the Academy of Sciences," he explained.

I took the lid from Bobby's hands. "I'll take it back and get you something nice." I had seen a special sale on cotton socks while I had been at the department store.

"But I like it," he began to rhapsodize. "Anyone can have a dog or a cat. But an alligator is something else. I even want to go to Florida to study them when I grow up. I always thought they were neat lying in the water at the academy. They look just like logs until you get too close. Then—snap!" He slapped his palms together in illustration.

I saw monster movies for the same reasons—and had a lot more fun and a lot less trouble. "But you hate violence. When a Western or a war movie comes on the TV, you always leave the room. One time you even made me turn off a cartoon."

He shrugged. "This is different. It's . . . it's natural."

"That's the point," I argued. "Movie violence is just fake. The blood's just Karo syrup and red dye." I nodded to the alligator. "These guys really do rip off arms." I added in case Mother was around, "When they're bigger."

"But that's real. Movies are somehow"—he hunted for the right words—"more than real. If an alligator gets a chicken, it happens in our world. In those war movies, I'm in someone else's world."

I didn't know my little brother had it in him. Maybe sweet little Bobby wasn't so sweet after all.

"Thanks a lot, Teddy." Bobby leaned over the box to pat my arm.

"Watch it!" I shoved him back before the alligator could gut him.

He misunderstood my rescue attempt. "Are you angry at me? I'm sorry that I ruined your surprise."

I couldn't stand it. Now he was apologizing. "Forget it," I snapped.

Suddenly he grinned from ear to ear. "I think I'll call him Teddy." He said it as if that were the only name for an alligator.

"I'm honored," I said, and added, "I think."

chapter five

Mother finally remembered to close the door. The room now stank of Mr. Wong's cough medicine. She skirted the box with the alligator and struggled with one of the windows. They were hard to open ever since the apartment had been painted last summer.

I hunted desperately for some excuse. I didn't want an alligator to be named after me. "Bobby, don't you think it will be a little confusing if there are two Teddys in the house?"

"Oh, I didn't think about that," Bobby said. He stared down at the alligator for a moment. The alligator stared back. "How about Oscar?"

"Perfect," I said. "Don't you think so, Mother?"

When Mother finally opened a window, she turned around. "You can't keep that thing in our house."

"But Teddy gave him to me," Bobby protested. "You don't want to hurt his feelings."

In fact, I had felt an immense sense of relief now that

Mother had put her foot down. "Maybe Mother's right. I didn't really think."

"No," Bobby insisted desperately. "It can be our pet together. You're always heading to the herpetology section."

It took me a moment to remember where in the academy I spent most of my time. "You mean the reptile area?"

"And the alligator pool." Bobby appealed to me as a potential ally. "You're always standing there."

I was just trying to figure out how to gather up all the shiny coins people throw among the alligators and not lose a hand. However, I didn't think I'd win any extra points telling the truth. "Where are we going to keep it? How are we going to feed it?"

Mother looked at me as if I should have thought of that before. "That's right. We don't know how to care for it."

"I can go to the library and get a book," Bobby said. "In the meantime, we make things as much like a swamp as we can."

Mother was offended. "My house is a clean house."

Bobby corrected himself quickly. "No, I mean, we can make it like the alligator pool. I know. We could keep it in a pan on top of the stove. The heat from the pilot light would keep the water warm."

Mother gazed doubtfully at Oscar's needle-sharp teeth. "But I need to cook on the stove."

"When you do, we'll move Oscar to the bathroom."
Bobby got up and went over to Mother. "Please,
Mother. Please."

I realized that I was now the nearest available gator
chow. So I got up hurriedly and joined them. "Father
would never let you keep it."

"That's right," Mother said quickly. "Father would
never allow an alligator in the house." But I could see
the wheels turning in her mind. She would let Father
play the villain and disappoint Bobby. "But we'll keep it
in the meantime and see what he says." She headed
for one of the closets. "I didn't get a chance to wrap
this yet. I hope it's okay." She brought out the turtle
island.

"That's perfect," Bobby said. He ran over to Mother
and gave her a hug. Then he looked at me affection-
ately. "You and Teddy had Oscar picked out from the
start, didn't you?"

"In a way," I said. After all, Oscar was a kind of cousin to a turtle.

Bobby scampered back with the island and set it on
the rug. "Oscar, this is your new home."

Before Mother or I could stop him, he reached in and
grasped Oscar right behind the head. Strangely, Oscar
didn't object. He just hung there in Bobby's hand.
"That's a boy." He stroked Oscar's yellow stomach with
a finger. I would have sworn Oscar wagged the tip of
his tail, as contented as any dog.

"It's just the right size," he said, eyeing the island critically. However, the moment he set Oscar on it, Oscar began to thrash his tail. Twisting his head, Oscar began to chomp at the plastic palm tree. It broke with a snap. He would have swallowed it if Bobby hadn't whisked the tree away. "Bad Oscar. Bad Oscar," he scolded as he wagged his finger.

Crouched in the plastic turtle home, Oscar's eyes followed Bobby's finger. Relative to Oscar's size, Bobby's finger probably looked like a whole roll of baloney.

Quickly I shoved Bobby's hand away. "He must be part goat," I said.

A frustrated Oscar began swinging his tail even harder. Cracks appeared in the plastic sides. Once I saw Oscar demolish the island, I was sorry that I had ever bought him for Bobby. The store clerk had been right. An alligator was no pet for a boy—not even for a goody-goody like Bobby.

"If you like an alligator, you'll like a turtle twice as much," I said. "Let me exchange it for you."

Bobby wrinkled his nose in disgust. "Not a chance. Turtles are slow and boring. There's no challenge to studying them. Oscar makes life interesting."

True enough. None of us realized just how interesting Oscar would make our lives.

chapter six

The alligator rested happily on the island as Bobby headed for the kitchen. I trailed along, feeling as if I were in a bad dream. Mother kept a safe distance behind the two of us.

Bobby took a step through the doorway and paused thoughtfully. "We need something flat and strong."

The kitchen was cluttered with Mother's party preparations. There were bowls of chopped onion and garlic and ginger, boned chicken cut into cubes, strips of beef and lamb, and rank after rank of spices. The wok sat ready on the stove.

I went to the lower cabinet by the stove and opened the doors. "Mother, do you need the cake pan?"

Mother gave me a dirty look. I had tipped her hand. "No, we already ordered something at Eastern Bakery." That was Bobby's favorite bakery. "Your father will pick it up on his way home."

I started to lift out the cake pan on top, but Mother

stopped me. "Get the old one." I took out the stack and found one that was blackened with use. I suppose Mother intended to throw it out after having an alligator live in it.

Bobby leaned his head to the side as his eyes measured his pet. "Put in about an inch of water."

Going to the sink, I filled up the pan and brought it over to the stove. I set it on the flat rectangular griddle between the burners. "Just move it when you need to cook," I told Mother.

"*You* will move it," Mother insisted.

When I stepped back, Bobby tipped the box and Oscar slid into the pan with a splash. He tilted up his snout expectantly.

"I think Oscar's hungry," Bobby said with the same conviction he used in naming his pet.

I had never been big on watching the nature shows like *Wild Kingdom.* All I could remember were Tarzan movies. The alligators usually had humans for snacks. Bobby, though, turned to Mother. "Can I have some raw meat, Mother?"

Mother had this dazed look as if this had already gone further than she had ever imagined. "Take some cut-up chicken."

"Perfect." Bobby searched the bowls on the table until he found the pale pink cubes of chicken. Selecting one, he held it over the pan.

"Careful," Mother and I said at the same time.

"Don't worry." As if he were an old hand at wrangling alligators, he held the chicken high over Oscar's head. Eyes intent, Oscar surged out of the water, forepaws held close to its chest. Its jaws snapped the air inches below the slice of raw chicken. It landed back with a splash in the water.

"Don't tease it," Mother said anxiously. "Those teeth look awfully sharp."

"I was just getting the range." Bobby held the slice of chicken lower. This time when Oscar rose from the pan, its jaws sank into the bottom half of the chicken. With a quick jerk of its head, it snatched the chicken from Bobby's fingers and fell back into the pan.

Oscar devoured the slice of chicken, opening and closing its jaws with a jerky motion. I watched in shock. Bobby watched in fascination. "Alligators like to stun their prey with their jaws. Other times, they sink their teeth into their victim and pull them under the water. The victim drowns, of course. Then they stash the body someplace underwater by the riverbank."

Nervously Mother pulled Bobby back. "Not so close."

I stared at Bobby as he stared at Oscar. "Where did you learn that stuff?"

"I read the information cards by the alligator pool." Bobby selected another piece of chicken and dangled it over the pan so Oscar could see the next course. Oscar's eyes followed the swaying slice of chicken. Did it imagine the slice was Tarzan swinging on a vine?

"Just throw the chicken in the water," Mother suggested. Like me, she was sure Bobby was going to lose a knuckle.

"Oscar wouldn't hurt me, would you, Oscar?" Bobby asked. The alligator responded by snatching the second piece and writhing in the pan.

"No, you wouldn't, would you?" There wasn't the least bit of affection in Oscar's cold, reptilian eyes, but from the way Bobby smiled, you would have thought Oscar had met Bobby at the door with his slippers.

Bobby kept feeding Oscar until the bowl was nearly half gone. Then I remembered something from my friend, Wayman, who had an aquarium. "Maybe alligators are like fish: as long as there's food they'll keep eating. They'll eat until they burst."

Bobby nodded his head. "That's probably true." He made an elaborate show of dusting off his hands. "All gone, boy."

As he washed his hands in the sink, I shook my head. "Oscar's not a dog."

"He's better than a dog," Bobby declared. "He's a watch alligator." He glanced over his shoulder at Oscar. "Aren't you, boy?"

Oscar clashed his jaws together as if in answer.

While Bobby gazed at his pet, Mother stepped out into the hallway. She crooked a finger at me. When I joined her, she folded her arms. "Well?"

"You said to get something special," I said defensively.

She arched an eyebrow. "What's the matter? Couldn't you afford a lion?"

"There was a waiting list," I cracked. "Ow." I rubbed the spot where Mother had rapped a knuckle.

"What's wrong with you?" Mother snapped. "Only a monster would give a monster as a present."

I looked back into the kitchen. My little brother was chatting with his alligator again in a soft, friendly voice. "Look at him. He loves it. He's the monster."

Mother swung me around to face her. "Why do you treat him this way? There's a Chinese proverb that says, 'Losing a brother is like losing a wing.' " Mother only spouted Chinese proverbs when she was upset.

"Well, we're American."

She folded her arms. "Even American brothers are supposed to be nice to one another."

I slouched against a wall. "He doesn't need me to be kind to him. Everyone likes him better than they like me."

Right about now I could have really used a hug. My parents, though, never showed their affection like the white parents on television. I wanted a hug so bad that it almost hurt.

Instead, Mother just fussed with my shirt collar. "That's not true."

Mother's words stung rather than comforted. I had seen the proof plenty of times. If we got into a fight, she always took Bobby's side and never mine. If she had a special treat, Bobby always got the first and biggest share. In fact, if I dropped off the face of the earth, no one would miss me.

"It is true," I insisted. "For one thing, everybody assumes the worst when I do something—even you. It's never Bobby's fault. He's Mr. Perfection."

Mother stiffened. "You think you're so smart, but this time you outsmarted yourself." She pointed to the refrigerator. "I've got five pounds of jumbo shrimp in there. Take out the veins."

Father worked in a fish store so he always got bargains on shrimp, crab, and fish. It wasn't really a vein in the shrimp but its stomach that sometimes still had black stuff in there. It was one of the messiest, smelliest jobs. Mother knew how much I hated it.

I groaned. "That'll take the whole afternoon."

Mother took me by the shoulders and propelled me back toward the kitchen. "And if you don't do a good job, I'll feed you to Oscar myself."

chapter seven

When Uncle Mat's family arrived, Bobby greeted them. "This way to the Everglades swamp," he said, and led them down the hallway into the kitchen. By now they knew enough to leave the presents and coats in our bedroom.

Both Uncle Mat and Aunt Martha were as curious as their daughter, Alice. "Swamp, what swamp?" Uncle Mat's voice boomed in the small hallway. Of all the barkers at the church bazaar, he was the only one who never needed a megaphone. His voice was always loud enough to cut across a crowded basement.

Mother seemed startled to hear her nice, spotless kitchen called a swamp. "Did the pipes burst again?" she asked.

Aunt Martha gave her a sympathetic peck. "It always happens on a holiday, doesn't it?"

Bobby proudly ushered our guests over to the stove. "This is Oscar. Isn't it neat-o?"

"I need my stove, Bobby," Mother said firmly.

Everyone gasped when he stretched over the pan to pick it up. Oscar, however, sat indifferently while its master lifted it up. "Don't worry, Mother. I've got everything ready."

As Bobby made his way out of the kitchen, Uncle Mat and Alice bumped one another, trying to get out of his way. "What's ready?" Mother demanded. When I just shrugged, she was the first to plunge after Bobby.

We were just in time to catch sight of him heading into the bathroom. Next to the bathtub he had placed a chair. Clamped to its back was Father's sunlamp. He called it his ninety-nine-cent vacation, and he used it to warm away his aches and pains from his job.

Bobby set the tray down in the bathtub. Then, with a flourish, he turned on the sunlamp. "Behold the relentless tropical sun!"

The hot red light poured down on the pan. Oscar slithered around with flicks of his tail. He looked as happy as I had ever seen him.

"Maybe you could keep that thing in here," Aunt Martha suggested.

Uncle Mat scowled. "Naw, you can't leave that light on all day and all night. It might short out. Maybe even start a fire."

Mother looked at the lamp as if it were about to explode. "It would?"

Uncle Mat thought a moment and announced, "But it's okay for the party."

Before anyone could stop him, Bobby leaned over the bathtub and grabbed Oscar around the trunk. With an expert twist of his wrist, he flipped Oscar onto its back. As Oscar began to thrash its tail and kick its legs, Bobby began to rub its belly. "I saw this on a nature show about alligator wrestlers."

Oscar's legs grew still, and his head and tail slipped back into the water. "See, he likes it," Bobby said.

"Let me try." Alice started for the bathtub.

Aunt Martha, though, blocked her. "Who ever heard of a surgeon with only one hand?"

"A doc that charges only half as much." Uncle Mat started to guffaw, but when he saw Aunt Martha's face he stopped. "I don't think you ought to do it anyway, honey," he mumbled to his daughter. "It might have germs."

Mother had something else to worry about now. "Germs?"

Bobby went on stroking Oscar's belly. "It's perfectly healthy, Mother."

It was hard to keep Uncle Mat down for long. "There's only enough to make one shoe," Uncle Mat said. "Are you going to make a coin purse?"

Bobby jumped to his feet indignantly. "It's my pet. Teddy gave it to me."

"Teddy, hunh?" Uncle Mat turned and shook his head at me. I hadn't fooled anyone—except Bobby. "You're a real kidder, aren't you?"

I squirmed, trying to think of a way to defend myself. Only I couldn't. However, it was Bobby who got me off the hook. Even now, my little brother hadn't gotten the real picture.

Bobby turned to me. "We had the neatest time feeding Oscar, didn't we, Teddy?"

In its pan, Oscar righted itself with a splash and clashed its jaws.

I smiled weakly and used Bobby's favorite word. "Neat-o."

chapter eight

The swamp drew everyone. All the guests had to see
Oscar: Aunt Norma, Aunt Ethel and Uncle Curtis, and
their daughter, Nancy. Even Grandmother went in to
see. Her eyes grew very wide, and she flapped her
hands at the wrists. "What is that thing?"

"An alligator," Bobby said. He tried to think of the
Chinese, but they hadn't taught that word in Chinese
school.

Uncle Curtis told her. He added, also in Chinese,
"They come from Africa."

"Florida," I said.

Uncle Curtis, though, believed he was the expert on
everything. "Do you subscribe to *National Geographic*?"
he demanded.

His wife, Aunt Ethel, always liked to tease him and
take him down a peg. "You don't bother with the
words. You just look at the pictures."

Since Aunt Ethel had already corrected her husband,

I thought it was safe to add, "I read it at the Academy of Sciences."

Really enjoying himself, Uncle Mat folded his arms and nodded. Though he was Uncle Curtis's brother, they were always trying to beat one another. He decided to get his own digs in. "I bet they know as much as an ambulance chaser."

Grandmother, though, got to the heart of things. "What is it doing here?"

"It's a pet," Bobby said. "Teddy gave it to me."

Grandmother wrinkled her forehead. "Why?"

"It's better than socks," suggested Uncle Curtis. Uncle Mat looked at his brother. "That's all I ever got from Mat. It's all I get now."

Uncle Curtis elbowed Uncle Mat's big gut. "Your feet are the only things that don't keep growing."

Grandmother turned and sidled in between her two boys. Though she was tiny, she shoved them apart easily. "Don't make fun of your brother," she said, and slapped Uncle Curtis's arm.

"Yeah," Uncle Mat said.

Annoyed, Grandmother turned. "You, too. Don't make fun." She thumped Uncle Mat's big belly. Then she looked at me. I wasn't afraid, though. She might hit her adult children, but she never struck her grandchildren.

"Now you," she said. "What kind of pet is this alligator?"

I remembered a birthday card I had seen but not bought. "It's a special present for a special boy."

I couldn't fool Grandmother. "You did it to make trouble."

To my immense embarrassment, Bobby leaped to my defense. "I think it's neat-o, Grandmother. If I could have thought of such a neat present, I would have asked for it." He grinned at me. "But I don't have Teddy's imagination." Bobby seemed puzzled by everyone else's negative reaction.

Grandmother wagged a finger at me. "Too much imagination makes for too much trouble."

The funny thing was that no one went very far after leaving the bathroom. Instead, they stayed in the hallway—even Grandmother. When a new guest came into the apartment, like Cousin Pam or Cousin Arnold, they would shout eagerly, "Hey, come on and see Bobby's gift. Hurry!"

It was even funnier that everyone knew whom to blame. "It's got to be Teddy, right?"

I felt myself sinking lower and lower. Bobby didn't help matters either. Before anyone could criticize me, he would blurt out, "I love my pet! Isn't it neat-o?"

Everyone in the crowd kept a respectful distance except Uncle Curtis, who was doing his best to study the alligator. Every now and then he would slip a gold pen from his shirt pocket and dig a little leather notebook out of his pants and jot something down.

Cousin Roderick was even more fearless. As soon as he came into the apartment, he plunged through the crowd. He would have put his nose next to Oscar's snout, but Bobby pulled him back. "Weird," he whispered, and glanced at me. "Where did you find it?"

By now I was beginning to get irritated. It almost seemed as if I were wearing a sign announcing that I had given it to Bobby. "How do you know it was me?"

Cousin Roderick smirked. "Everybody else in this family gives practical presents: socks, shirts, blouses, or sweaters."

In the hallway, Grandmother overheard us and couldn't resist the chance to reinforce her warning. "Too much imagination makes for too much trouble."

"Not this time, Grandmother," Bobby explained.

It's bad enough to get caught at playing a prank, but when the victim defends you, you feel even lower than a bug. I decided that I was tired of being insulted. Cousin Roderick was my age so we often did things together. "I got a new tape," I said. "Want to listen to it?"

"Later." Cousin Roderick leaned his head to study the alligator from another angle. "I want to look at Bobby's pet."

I stared at him in surprise. "But it's your favorite group." Besides, he never referred to Bobby by name. Bobby was always "the twerp."

Cousin Roderick waved an irritated hand at me. "I

can always hear them on the radio. How often do I get to see an alligator in my cousin's bathtub?"

That was true enough—so true that I didn't know how to argue. Seeing that Cousin Roderick hadn't lost any limbs, our other cousins slipped into the bathroom. For once, Bobby was the center of attention as they asked him questions. Some of them Bobby could answer because he had read about alligators at the academy, but others he couldn't.

"What does it eat?" Cousin Roderick finally asked.

"Meat," Uncle Curtis supplied. "Look at those sharp teeth. It's no herbivore."

"Have you fed it yet?" Cousin Roderick asked.

"We gave it lunch, but then we stopped because we didn't want to overfeed it," Bobby explained.

Cousin Roderick grinned. "Well, it's din-din time now. Let's go to the kitchen and borrow some more meat."

All the children slipped through the adults chatting in the hallway. In the kitchen, Mother was busy at the stove. "Mother, can I feed Oscar again?" Bobby asked.

Mother was in the middle of deciphering a recipe on a worn index card so she said absently, "Sure. Just don't let it spoil your appetite."

It was obvious she hadn't heard us. Under normal circumstances, Bobby might have been more careful, but he wasn't used to being the center of attention, and he was always eager to please everyone. So he grabbed the bowl filled with the rest of the raw chicken. "Thanks," Bobby said. "You're the best, Mother."

I had a hunch that Mother wouldn't have approved. However, if Oscar starved to death, I wouldn't get any refund. So instead, I kept quiet as Bobby led the others out of the kitchen.

chapter nine

As the owner, Bobby got to pick the first piece. All of us children squeezed around the bathtub. In the hall, the adults crowded around the doorway to stare.

Uncle Curtis paused long enough in his scientific observations to warn us, "Careful of your fingers."

"Come on, boy. Come on," Bobby coaxed. He held the chicken carefully above his pet's head.

From the pan, Oscar was just two slitted golden eyes staring up at the dangling meat.

"Dinnertime," Bobby urged.

In the blink of an eye, Oscar suddenly reared up, neck straining, jaws stretched open to reveal rows of tiny, vicious teeth. Its jaws clamped on a cube of raw meat. With a twist of its head, Oscar snatched the chicken from Bobby's grasp and then splashed back into the pan.

Bobby didn't even notice that his shirt was wet. The adults were murmuring in wonder. Cousin Roderick said out loud to no one in particular, "Did you see it grab that chicken? I'm glad that wasn't my finger."

"Can I feed it?" Cousin Alice asked.

"Then me," Cousin Nancy chimed in.

As the youngest, Bobby's opinions usually didn't count. Today, though, Bobby handled his new importance well. First, he carefully counted up the cubes of chicken. Then he assigned each of them a number. When he had run through the cousins, he was going to start over, but the adults demanded a turn—even Grandmother.

When she got to hold the chicken over the pan, Oscar obediently opened its mouth. With a yelp, Grandmother dropped the chicken into its jaws. "Just like feeding Matthew when he was a baby," she observed, and everyone laughed, even Uncle Mat.

Bobby beamed, the center of attention.

After everyone had had a turn, there was one piece of chicken left. "You haven't had a chance," he said, and offered me the bowl.

"It's your birthday," I said.

"Go on," he said, and held the bowl out.

In the pan, Oscar thrashed his tail. It was strange, but suddenly I had an urge to experience what everyone else had. I took the cube of chicken and held it over the pan. I flicked the chicken back and forth. Staring up at my hand, Oscar squatted in the water. When it opened its jaws, I felt a little thrill as I saw

44

the rows of small, needle-sharp teeth. The cold golden orbs of its eyes stared at my hand as hungrily as they had at the first piece of chicken. Oscar would have cheerfully eaten chicken, fingers, and hand if it could. I felt the same kind of thrill I did when I went on the roller coaster out at Playland—just as it topped the initial rise before it roared down for the first time.

Oscar was so strange, so different. Suddenly I understood the others' excitement. I spread my thumb and fingers apart, and the chicken dropped like a moist bomb. Oscar's head swung, but too late. The meat plopped into the water, where it floated.

As lithe as a snake, Oscar wriggled around, and its jaws closed on the hapless piece of chicken. Raising its snout out of the water, Oscar opened and shut its jaws on the chicken as if stunning the little pink cube of meat. Oscar seemed to take particular satisfaction in that last piece. With startled cries, everyone jumped back—everyone, that is, except Bobby.

"He really likes you," Bobby said. "I can tell."

"It takes one cold-blooded critter to know another," Uncle Curtis teased. He was always telling dumb jokes.

"Then it really ought to like a lawyer," Uncle Mat teased.

As Grandmother called for silence, we could hear Mother call from the kitchen. "Has anyone seen the blue bowl? I've looked all over for it."

"Bobby's got it," Uncle Mat said quickly. He didn't want to get into trouble with his sister-in-law.

Bobby stood there helplessly with the empty bowl in his hands.

For once, my little brother had not been perfect. I had lived for this moment, but now that it had come and I saw his face, I felt bad.

Anyway, if something went wrong, I usually got the blame. Why stop when you're batting a thousand?

Reaching over, I grabbed the bowl from him and pushed through the crowd. "I took it," I said.

Uncle Curtis defended us. "What's the fuss all about? There's beef. There's shrimp."

"I brought black mushrooms," Grandmother added, and announced to all of us, "They cost five dollars a pound." Mother said she did that so we would appreciate the present more. However, we were not supposed to do that when we bought a gift for someone.

"But Harold likes cashew chicken so," Mother fretted.

Aunt Norma had begun rummaging around in the refrigerator. "Let's see what else you've got in the icebox. Here's some old bean curd." She took out a package and sniffed it. "It still smells good."

"Didn't I bring that to you last week?" Aunt Ethel asked. She was always bringing over things she thought were good for us. Other guests brought candy; she brought turnips.

Grandmother clapped her hands together once and held out her palms. "Give that to me. I'll fix it."

Everyone pitched in then. Usually when we got together, we all helped out, but Oscar had distracted us.

Vegetables got sliced. Garlic got chopped. Ginger got shaved into thin strips.

In no time, Mom was so busy supervising her helpers that she forgot about the missing chicken.

Grandmother herself took over cooking the cashew chicken, which had plenty of water chestnuts, bamboo shoots, and cashews. When she was finished with it, the bean curd looked sort of like chicken.

The other adults acted like guilty little kids. With a wink, Aunt Norma whisked the bowl from me and washed it, and Uncle Curtis dried it, and Uncle Mat put it away on a high shelf where Mother would not see it.

chapter ten

Mother had timed dinner so we could eat as soon as
Father closed up the store. That wouldn't be until nine
o'clock. Then it would take him a half hour to lock up
and walk up the hill to home.

Chinatown stays up late. The grocery stores are open
until nine, and the souvenir shops and restaurants
keep their doors open even later. As a result, family life
begins late. Some nights when Mother and Father were
too tired to cook, we would go out to a restaurant.
There we would see other families who had stores or
shops along Grant Avenue. Sometimes Bobby and I did
not get to bed before midnight.

We were so busy cooking that we didn't hear Father
come home. The first thing we heard were his heavy
work shoes clunking on the floor.

Mother looked at the Hires root beer clock. It had
once hung in Aunt Norma's grocery store, but Mother
had got it when our old cat-shaped clock had broken.

"That sounds like your father, but it can't be. It's not even nine."

Uncle Mat cupped his hands around his mouth like a megaphone. "If it's burglars, she keeps her jewelry in the first drawer of the bureau in the bedroom."

"Shut up, Mat." Mother slapped her brother-in-law's arm. "Harold, is that you?"

"I swear," he grumbled, "people get crazier every year. I caught this little old lady pinching the crabs to see if they were fresh. I said, 'That's it. I'm going home.' So I closed the store early," Father said from the hallway. "I'll be with you in a minute."

"We have to warn your father about Oscar." Mother urgently elbowed Uncle Mat out of the way and hurried toward the hall. She stopped when she heard Father shout. "Too late," she sighed.

You could have heard Father's yell across the bay. He came running to the kitchen doorway. "Holy moly, there's a dinosaur in the bathtub!"

"You didn't scare it, did you, Father?" Anxiously, Bobby slid around him and into the hall.

"It's only a little baby," Aunt Ethel scolded Father. "Shame on you." She followed Bobby to the bathroom.

"You could have scared the growth right out of it," Uncle Mat added as he also went into the hallway. Cousins Alice and Nancy trailed after him.

His pride hurt, Father called after them, "I'm all right, everyone. Don't worry about me."

Mother tried to soothe him as she patted his arm. "Of course, we were worried about you, Harold. But we were also worried about Oscar. After all, this is a strange new place to him."

"It's pretty odd to me, too." Father was still in the tan smock he wore in the store. He dug around in his many pockets among the pens, grease pencils, and slips of paper until he found a handkerchief. He used it to wipe his forehead. "Now will someone tell me who's Oscar?"

Cousins Alice and Nancy came back to announce, "Oscar was so upset, he was thrashing around, but Bobby's calming him down."

"Who's Oscar?" Father demanded.

Normally we would have answered Father right away, but our cousins' news flash concerned us all. "Bobby's not trying to pet it, is he?" Mother said with a frown.

"Oh, he's got him on his back so it's all right," Cousin Alice assured her.

Father stood in front of Mother. "Will you please tell me who in the world Oscar is?"

However, Mother was so distracted that she just moved Father out of the way. "In a minute, dear."

Father was so surprised, he just watched as our other relatives paraded by after Mother. In the end, it was only Grandmother, Uncle Curtis, Father, and I.

Father turned to Uncle Curtis in silent appeal.

"Who's Oscar, and what's a crocodile doing in our bathroom?"

Uncle Curtis had been busy jotting in his little notebook. "Actually, it's an alligator."

Grandmother clanged her spoon noisily on the side of the wok. "And that's no bathtub," Grandmother declared. "It's the swamp." She winked at me. She liked to have her own private jokes with her grandchildren.

In desperation, Father finally fixed on me. "Swamp? What swamp?"

Mother gave his shoulder a pat as she came back. "It's just Mat's little joke. Don't let it upset you."

Father whirled around. "And the crocodile?"

Uncle Curtis looked up from his notebook for a moment. "Alligator."

Father was just as confused as ever. "Who's Oscar, then?"

Mother crouched slightly as she began to heat up the soup. "Oscar is the crocodile."

"Alligator," Uncle Curtis corrected her.

Father snatched the notebook from Uncle Curtis and flung it into a corner. "Who cares? I want to know what a green scaly thing is doing in my bathtub."

Uncle Curtis calmly took out another notebook and began writing again. "Nothing much when you're not scaring it."

Father stretched his arms out and then let his hands

slap his sides. "Will someone please tell me how my bathroom got turned into a zoo?"

"It's all quite simple, dear. Oscar is Bobby's pet," Mother explained as she checked the rest of the dinner. "We had to put it somewhere so I could cook dinner."

"Pet?" Father was more puzzled than ever. "Who said Bobby could have a pet, and who said the pet could be a crocodile? I mean," he added as Uncle Curtis opened his mouth to correct him, "an alligator?"

Mother shrugged. "Well, no one said he could have an alligator. It just sort of . . . happened."

Like Grandmother, Father knew who had too much imagination and just whom he should blame. He turned to me. "Was this your idea? Did you talk your brother into it?"

I did my best to look industrious by heading for the drawer to get the chopsticks. "Mother said I could get him a turtle."

Father planted his fists on his hips. "What did you do? Give it vitamins?"

I began to set the chopsticks out in pairs. It seemed like the only time Father paid attention to me was when I had done something wrong. Just once I wished he could have said something nice like the American fathers did on television.

"It was on special," I said.

Father rubbed the back of his neck. "I can see why.

Only crazy people would bring a monster into the house."

Uncle Curtis put away his notebook. "Don't be such a pill. Your kids can learn something about science."

"It's neat-o," Grandmother added.

Education, though, was the magical word. Father looked around the kitchen and then listened to the noise from the bathroom. "Oscar certainly has made a big impression on everyone." He gave a grunt. "I guess he can stay for a while."

chapter eleven

"You were always cranky when you were hungry," Grandmother said. She banged her spoon on the side of the wok. It rang like a gong.

Grandmother knew Father. He perked up when he smelled dinner. His shoulders straightened and he started to smile. "You're right, Mama."

I thought I'd add to Father's good mood. "You're going to like this."

His eyes shone when he saw the cashew chicken. "I've been dreaming about this all day. Mr. Ong, the florist, wanted to treat me to a big lunch, but I said, 'No way. I'm saving my appetite for my wife's cashew chicken.' "

Before I could stop him, he had grabbed a big cooking spoon and dipped it into the wok. "We had to change the recipe a little," I tried to warn him.

"It smells the same," Father said, and stuck the

spoon into his mouth. He put up a hand like a screen before his full mouth. "It tastes the same, too."

Lowering his hand, he began to chew. After a moment, he stopped smiling. After another moment, he paused. He tried an experimental chew. He drew his eyebrows together in puzzlement. He directed a silent question at his mother.

"It's bean curd," Grandmother said. As Father's eyes bulged and his back stiffened in indignation, Grandmother wagged a finger at him. "It's good for you."

Lifting his head, his neck muscles strained. You'd think he was swallowing a poisoned boulder. "I hate bean curd," Father said. "It's too mushy."

"It's got as much protein as chicken," Uncle Curtis informed him.

Father shot a poisonous look at Uncle Curtis, but before he could open his mouth, Grandmother warned him. "No bad language." She nodded in my direction so I tried to cooperate by looking as innocent as I could.

Frowning, Father turned to the wok and fished around with the spoon. Lifting out one of the chunks, he held it directly under the kitchen light so he could examine the sample. "What happened to the chicken?"

Grandmother took the spoon away from him. "Your boy's watching. Set a good example. No tantrums, now."

I didn't want Father getting any madder so I tried to be helpful. When he started to reach around behind his back, I darted in and untied his smock's cloth belt for him.

Father stood patiently while I undid the knot. "I bought the chicken myself," he groused. "I just want to know where it went."

Grandmother shook some gravy from the spoon into the wok. "We gave it the night off."

Since Grandmother wouldn't give him a straight answer, Father stared at me as he shrugged off his smock.

I made a point of lowering my eyes. When I had the smock in my hands, I pivoted right away and hung it on the knob of the back door.

Father, though, followed me. "I don't know how, but the bean curd has to be your doing."

I knew that look from before so I started to edge for the doorway and a quick getaway. "It's not my fault. We all did it—even Uncle Curtis."

Uncle Curtis knew his brother. That's why Uncle Curtis slipped beyond Father's reach, too. "It was for science."

Exasperated, Father demanded, "Curtis, what's scientific about cashew chicken? Do I go over to your house and experiment on your dinner?"

Uncle Curtis was standing right by me now, ready to shove me out of his way. "You're welcome to, anytime."

"The alligator was hungry." Grandmother patted Father on the shoulder. "Now get the rice bowls from the cupboard."

Father, though, was too amazed to obey. "You took perfectly good chicken from my mouth and gave it to that monster instead?"

Uncle Curtis quietly tried to slip behind me, but I wouldn't let him use me as a shield. "For crying out loud, Harold, there's plenty of other meat to eat."

Father grumbled, "Only because I came home when I did."

He might have said more, but Grandmother poked him with the spoon. "Make yourself useful. Get the rice bowls."

"I'll help you," I said. As he turned to the cupboards, though, I could see the gravy stain the spoon had left on his shirt.

As Father took the stacks of rice bowls from the shelf, he studied me. I did my best to be busy so he couldn't question me right away.

Next we arrayed the chopsticks in pairs, setting them out in the pattern of a fan. Just as we were putting out the soup spoons, Mother led the others back into the kitchen. "I hope this isn't what I think it is." She held out a long, flat pink box as if it were a corpse.

Father set the last of the spoons on the kitchen table. "I had it in my hands when I opened the bathroom door."

Because there was no room for it on the table, I drew out a kitchen chair.

Mother set the box down on the chair seat and lifted off the lid. Father had dropped the cake on its top. The icing and cake were more like mush now. "It's ruined," Mother said in dismay. She dropped the lid on the floor.

Grandmother was the practical one in the family. "So?" Grandmother asked. "It will get mixed up in your stomach. We just scoop up enough for each person." She passed the kitchen spoon to Mother like a sentry exchanging a rifle with her replacement.

I picked up the lid from the floor and made my way around Uncle Curtis. "What kind of idiot takes a cake into the bathroom?" he asked Father. Uncle Curtis *really* liked his desserts.

Father glared back. "What kind of idiot feeds a birthday dinner to a monster?"

Uncle Mat had been a restaurant cook at one time so he helped Mother finish the last preparations. "There are plenty of other dishes. Don't be such a crybaby."

Father pointed in the direction of the bathroom. "I don't work all day just to feed that . . . that walking wallet."

Aunt Ethel began setting out the big bowls for the different dishes. "How can a big man like you pick on an itty-bitty thing like that?"

"It's got teeth," Father said.

Aunt Ethel waved a bowl at Father. "Your teeth are bigger."

As I folded up the lid and mashed it into the garbage can, I saw Father's legs bending. He was so mad that he was going to sit down without checking.

"Watch out!" I called.

Too late. Father sat down. He didn't say anything at first. He just squirmed a little bit. The sides of the cake box had collapsed beneath him into a flat pink platform. Aunt Norma chuckled. "Did you hatch anything, Harold?"

However, Father did not reply. With as much dignity as he could muster under the circumstances, he pinched the sides of his gooey pants and held them away from his legs as he slowly rose.

His pants were a mishmash of chocolate cake and white icing. I could still make out a red squiggle of lettering in reverse: HAP . . . BOB . . .

"I hope there's ice cream," Uncle Mat said. "Or did you sit on that, too?"

I grabbed a dish towel and went over to Father. "Let me clean that."

Still, Father said nothing. First, he contemplated the destroyed birthday cake. Then he pondered the chickenless cashew chicken in the wok.

I started to dab at his leg, but he waved me off. Then, in his sticky pants, Father waddled over to Bobby. "This is all that monster's fault. We've lost a cake and a chicken. You are not to waste good food on that thing anymore. Good food is for humans. Let it eat garbage."

"But Harold—," Mother started to protest.

"That's my final word," Father declared. "And now I'm going to change my clothes." Even Grandmother knew when not to argue with her stubborn son. Silently we parted to either side as Father awkwardly walked out through the doorway.

chapter twelve

"Don't say anything," Mother coached us.

"Right." Uncle Curtis playfully punched Bobby in the shoulder. "There'll be plenty of garbage after the party. Enough to take care of ten alligators."

Bobby, though, was a born worrier. During the rest of the party, he was like a zombie. He just went through the motions of eating and present unwrapping.

His heart wasn't in it. As always, Uncle Mat and Aunt Martha gave him a sensible white shirt. He showed as much enthusiasm for it as he did for the Willie Mays glove Uncle Curtis and Aunt Ethel bought him.

He didn't even bother opening the ly-cee Grandmother gave him. Grandmother always got the kind with a design of children printed on it. Inside she always put some money, depending on what she had won at her club.

Every Wednesday she played mah-jongg. It was like gin rummy but with tiles.

Sometimes, if she'd had bad luck, we'd only get fifty cents because Mrs. Eng had cheated. Once, though, it was five dollars. It really didn't matter because Mother always collected it and put it in the bank for college. Still, we were always curious about Grandmother's luck.

That night, though, Bobby just handed it mechanically to Mother. Later, when everyone was gone and we were in our bedroom, he watched me pound a fist into his mitt.

"Do you like it?" he asked.

Even if I did like it—and I did—I would never admit it. Instead, I just shrugged. "It's okay."

"I'll sell it to you," he said.

I rolled onto my side and looked at him for the first time. "How much?"

"That's a new mitt," he said, trying to bargain.

I took off the mitt and threw it to him. "It doesn't matter anyway. Oscar took all my money. I don't have anything left."

Bobby just stared at the mitt on his stomach. "Do you know anyone who would buy it?"

"You've pestered everyone for the last month to get you a mitt," I said.

"I've got to feed Oscar," Bobby said.

"There'll be plenty of garbage," I said.

"But what if there isn't?" he asked.

I sat up. "You're really worried about him." I didn't think anyone could get attached to that thing. That's what comes of watching too much public television.

"He's my pet," Bobby said.

"He's an alligator," I pointed out. "He'd bite off your thumb if you let him."

Bobby shrugged. "There are times you'd bite off my head if you could. Even so, I still love you."

"Yeah, well, I guess there is some gator in me," I said, startled.

I remembered all those times I had picked on—I mean, helped build Bobby's character. I thought he hadn't lost his temper because he was stupid. But he actually knew what was going on.

"Then why don't you get mad?" I asked.

He lay on his stomach. "Maybe because it takes someone like me to handle our friends—and someone like you to handle our enemies."

I guess it wasn't his fault if people liked him better than they liked me. "It's handy how that works out, isn't it?"

"I didn't hurt your feelings, did I?" he asked anxiously.

Considering what I had done to him in the past, his sensitivity only made me feel worse. "Not Gator Boy. My hide's too thick."

He could see right through me, though. "I'm sorry,

Teddy. I shouldn't have said anything. It's just that I'm worried about feeding Oscar."

I recalled how he had defended me at the party. I ought to be just as big as my little brother. "If you're really worried about finding enough food, there are plenty of restaurants in Chinatown. Oscar will eat better than us."

Bobby began to fret again. "Don't they usually keep the cans locked up?"

Like Bobby said, a gator-type person has his uses, too. "I'll go with you on your original expedition," I offered.

For the first time in a long time, he smiled. "You will?"

"I gave you the pet, so I'll help you once." I rolled over onto my back.

Relieved, Bobby picked up his mitt. "Thanks, Teddy."

"Time to go to bed, boys," Mother said.

When I woke up the next morning, I saw that Bobby had slept with the mitt on his hand the whole night.

"Come on," I said as I got out of bed. "Get up. Don't give Father any reason to get mad. We want him to cool off as soon as he can."

Bobby blinked sleepily. "Right."

I got dressed hurriedly and then checked on Bobby. I wanted to see what was taking him so long. He was still so sleepy that he was trying to pull his pajama top over his glove.

It took a couple of minutes to untangle him, get the mitt off, and put the right clothes on him. Mama had saved some special tidbits from the garbage so Bobby could feed Oscar. "But first you clean up after it."

As I looked at the pan, a new thought occurred to me. "How do you do that?"

"Carefully," Bobby said. He borrowed a bowl from Mama. Somehow he managed to catch Oscar behind its head. When Bobby lifted his pet out of the pan, Oscar wriggled, spraying the kitchen with water.

Depositing Oscar in a bowl, Bobby put a plate over the top to keep his pet inside. As he went to wash the pan and change the water, the plate began to clack up and down. Mama nudged me, and I put my hands on the plate to keep Oscar inside.

As I stood guard, Mama whispered in my ear. "You can buy me a new bowl for Christmas."

"I'll buy one sooner than that," I promised.

chapter thirteen

We attended St. Mary's Grammar School even though we weren't Catholic. During the day, there was an hour of instruction in the Chinese language that our parents wanted us to have. There were a lot of non-Catholics who attended for the same reason. When I got there, my friend Ollie was standing by the gate that led down the steps into the courtyard. "You didn't."

I guess that sweet Cousin Roderick had been busy on the telephone last night. "I didn't do a lot of things."

Since I wasn't helping any, Ollie turned to Bobby, who was walking by my side. "Did he?"

Bobby looked over his shoulder to see if Ollie was talking to someone behind him. As far as I could re-member, it was the first time that Ollie had ever recog-nized that Bobby existed. When Bobby realized Ollie was talking to him, he said, "He did."

"I did," I confessed.

"And you got your fingers?" Ollie demanded.

Bobby put down his book bag and held up both hands.

"Can I see it?" Ollie asked.

I saw our chance. "You can even help us feed it," I said.

Ollie leaned his head back. "I can?"

I put my arm around Ollie's shoulder. "You see, we've got this little problem." And I explained what had happened last night. "This is just temporary. We have to give my father time to get over it."

"But to go through garbage." Ollie made a face.

"It needs a lot of food," I said.

Ollie's imagination began working overtime. "Just how big is this alligator, anyway?"

I thought I had him then. "Let me put it this way. You have to be a certain height or we can't let you near it." I held my hand palm down at about Bobby's height.

That last bit was too much. He leaned his head to the side and looked at me suspiciously. "I read *Tom Sawyer*, too. Get someone else to help you whitewash your fence," he said, and left us.

I tried everything I knew to get some volunteers. I appealed to their school spirit, to their patriotism, to their love of science. Even outright bribery did not work. No one wanted to root through the garbage.

So, after Chinese school, it was just Bobby and me.

"Okay, we want to do this quick and easy. I've given the matter some thought. We don't want to hit the real restaurants where we eat. We want to hit the tourist joints where you pay more for the cloth napkins and tablecloths than for the food."

"Tourists are hungry," Bobby argued.

"But they're too fussy so they never finish their meals." I spun him around and headed him down the hill. "Come on. We've got an alligator to feed."

It was late in the afternoon, and the tourists were still out. Most of them wore T-shirts and shorts. Even though they were shivering, they tried to pretend it was hot in San Francisco.

We ran past the clothing stores that sold more T-shirts. Like the ghosts of kites, the white rectangles hung in the windows. We scooted in front of the souvenir stores with the racks of postcards and plastic back scratchers. What they had to do with Chinatown I never knew.

When we came to the ricksha, I made Bobby stop. A ricksha was a kind of chair with wheels and an awning. There were two poles in front. I had always assumed the space was for a horse even though it was so narrow. Finally I asked Father about it one day, and he said that it was for a man. They used them in China, but he had never heard of one operating in San Francisco.

The ricksha stood in front of a door. On it were

painted funny towers that father said were pagodas. Like the ricksha, they had them in China but not here.

To the left was a huge picture window. Its wooden frame had been carved like bamboo. Through it, you could see all the tables covered with pink cloths. At each setting was a pink napkin and forks. The only people inside were more tourists in T-shirts and shorts.

Suddenly a woman stepped out from behind the cash register and came outside. She wore one of those old Chinese dresses. The side was split so you could see her chubby legs. "Go away," she said. "Don't sell your raffle tickets here. You can't pester my customers."

"The raffle was last month," I said. "We just wanted to know if you had any scraps of meat or fat or gristle."

The woman reared back as if I had said she wore them in her hair. "Go away. I don't have garbage either."

"Let's go." Bobby came along when I tugged him. "The food's lousy here anyway."

The woman glared at us as we left. When we heard a door slam, I figured she had gone inside. Still, we walked on.

"Hey," a man said. When we kept moving, he said again, "Hey, boy."

I turned to see an old Chinese. His hair had been cropped close to his head, and his mouth was filled with gold crowns. He wore a white shirt with the sleeves rolled up. A wet apron hung around his neck. "You understand Chinese, don't you?" he asked in Chinese.

"A little," I said.

He squinted at us as if his eyes were bad. "You're Blessed Strength's boy, aren't you? Your father brought you into our club, right?" Blessed Strength was father's Chinese name. Uncle Mat was Blessed Intelligence. Uncle Curtis was Blessed Charity. Blessed was the Chinese name that belonged to their generation. Strength was Father's personal name. However, everyone, even Grandmother, used his American name, Harold.

Only the old-timers called him Blessed Strength. They used Chinese names whenever they could. If Bobby or I tried to use English with them, they would nag us. If they saw us drinking soda, they would scold us for not drinking hot tea. They could make you feel like a criminal over the silliest things. So usually I stayed away from them.

"Yes," I answered in Chinese. "What about it?"

"I was taking a break," he said, and held up his cigarette. "I overheard you. If you want to go through the trash cans, you don't go to the Empress. She's just the hostess. She's just in charge of the customers. On matters of garbage, you come to the Duke of Scraps." He tapped his chest.

I glanced at the door, but we were standing at an odd angle to it. I didn't think the woman could see us, or maybe she was was busy inside. "May we go through your garbage?"

"What for?" he demanded.

"It's for our alligator."

The Duke of Scraps blinked a couple of times. Then, because he wanted to be sure, he asked us in English, his mouth having trouble with all the syllables. I answered in Chinese but had to use English for *alligator*.

He shook his head sadly—though I couldn't understand why. "Of course." He raised his hand and waved us down the alley.

As we walked, I whispered to Bobby. "Use Chinese. We don't need a sermon right now."

The cans were dented and dirty and greasy. I set my schoolbag down in a spot that looked pretty clean. "You take that can on the left," I said to Bobby.

A door suddenly opened, and another old-timer in an apron came out. With him came a gust of frying oil and sweet-and-sour sauce and soapsuds. "Hey, what do you want here?"

"They're Blessed Strength's boys, okay?" The Duke of Scraps strolled up to the door. "They asked the Empress if they could go through our garbage, and she ordered them away. Can you imagine that?"

The second old-timer drew himself up indignantly. "We ought to walk out and let her wash all the dishes herself."

The Duke of Scraps tried to chuckle but wound up coughing. "She'd break every fingernail and every plate."

"It'd serve her right," the second old-timer added. "Go on, boys. Take anything you want." He lifted the lids. Both cans looked pretty gross inside.

Bobby and I took off our sweaters and rolled up our shirtsleeves. We had saved our lunch bags, and we unfolded them now.

Then we got to work. I'll spare you the details in case you're eating while you read this. Let me just say that garbage duty is not for the squeamish.

As we hunted for scraps of meat, though, I could hear the Duke and his sidekick whisper to one another. I caught only snatches of their conversation. One said that it was sad. The other agreed. I missed most of his comments, but I heard something about business being bad.

I thought they were talking about their restaurant, and I felt sorry for them. When I had some scraps, I stood up. "How're you doing?"

"Great." Bobby held up his bag. "I've got a regular feast."

That set the two old-timers to another quick session of sad headshakes and whispers. The second old-timer went inside, and I saw him dialing a telephone. At the same time, the Duke pointed down the alley. "Go over to the Palace restaurant over on Jackson, okay?"

The Palace was another fancy tourist place. "No thank you," I said politely. "We've got enough."

"You go," the Duke ordered us sternly. "Don't worry. Someone will be waiting." He pointed toward the second old-timer who was on the telephone. I guess he was calling ahead.

Since the man belonged to Father's club, I was afraid to disobey. The Duke might complain to Father. Father was old-fashioned enough to expect us to treat a club member as a kind of uncle.

We slipped back along Grant and crossed Washington. The Palace was painted a gaudy red and green. Overhead, the neon chopsticks were already flashing on and off. Inside were more tourists in shorts and T-shirts eating at tables with green tablecloths and candles in squat red glass holders. It was the kind of place where they hid the soy sauce containers and put out sugar for the tea.

It's funny, though. No matter how fancy or silly the front, the kitchen in back always looks the same. And no matter what costumes the waiters may wear, the old-timers in the kitchen dress the same. Beneath their stained aprons, they wear white T-shirts and sensible gray work pants and heavy, comfortable work shoes.

Waiting in the Palace kitchen was a man with pre-sorted scraps fresh from the cutting table. They were already in a yellow plastic shopping bag with an ugly red drawing of Chinatown on it. When he presented the bag to us, he instructed us to go on to a third restaurant where yet another club member would be waiting. Once again, it was impossible to refuse.

By the time we were finished, we had a half dozen shopping bags.

chapter fourteen

"I'm tired," Bobby complained.

"Keep walking," I puffed. Between our schoolbags and the garbage, we had quite a load to carry up the hill.

"If Oscar eats all this, he'll explode. And we can't fit it all in the refrigerator," Bobby panted. "What do we do?"

My own arms ached. "Feed as much as you can to Oscar. We'll save what we can and throw away the rest."

At Powell, we had to wait for the cable car to rattle by. One tourist risked getting his head bashed in to photograph us. "Aren't they cute?" he said, and leaned far out from the running board to take a one-handed shot.

I guess we must have been downwind from them.

When we got home, Cousin Roderick, Ollie, and

some of the others were sitting on the steps. "Can we feed your alligator?"

I had just gone through a dozen trash cans and carried garbage up a hill. "Get lost. You wouldn't help us."

Bobby, though, was the forgiving sort. "It's okay." He was happy to be the center of attention again.

"Here, let me give you a hand." Ollie took one of Bobby's garbage bags. In no time, Bobby's hands were free to get out his key to our apartment.

However, I still had my full load. "I could use some help." But everyone was too busy scampering up the steps after Bobby. No one heard me.

"Traitors," I muttered. Grumbling, I followed the herd up the stairs. On the wall at the top of the stairs was a big lever that opened the front door. By the time I reached it, I could already hear Bobby divvying up some of the scraps.

Dropping my schoolbag in the hallway, I carried the rest of my burden into the kitchen. The refrigerator already looked pretty full when I opened the door.

At that moment, Mother came in through the back door. In her arms was a clothes basket. I guess she had been hanging laundry on the clotheslines up on the roof.

She sniffed the air. "What's that smell?"

"We got some scraps." I tried to fit a bag on a refrigerator shelf, but Mother snatched it away from me.

"You can't bring garbage into my house. Throw it out."

"It took so much work to get it," I said.

Mother was much more patient than my friend's mothers, but even she had her breaking point. "You have taken a cake pan. You have taken one of my good bowls. But not my refrigerator. Take it out."

So I took my bags of hard-won garbage down to the trash cans. Our can was full so I checked the landlord's can. There was plenty of room. He was probably too stingy to throw out anything.

I stuffed my bags into the can. As I climbed the steps, I met Bobby. His arms were loaded with his garbage bags. "Mama chased everyone out."

I made way for him on the stairs. "Well, you know where to go tomorrow. You can rotate: one restaurant a day."

When I was back upstairs, I went into the bathroom to wash my hands. Inside the tub, a plump Oscar floated in his pan, his eyes poking above the water, his little legs floating like dead sticks. "Sometimes," I muttered to myself, "I'm so smart I outsmart myself."

For once, I was grateful to have homework. It was a good distraction from recent events. Bobby usually joined me, but I guess he was observing his alligator. I was just describing the Council of Trent when the front door slammed, and I mean really slammed. I would have been surprised if it was still on its hinges.

Out in the hallway, I heard Mother ask, "What are you doing home so early?"

"Where are they?" Father sounded anguished.

"Where are who?" Mother wondered.

"Those . . . those murderers! Those assassins!" Father stormed. I decided to stay inside the room.

"Who got killed?"

The bedroom door banged open. "They killed our good name. It'll spread all over Chinatown." Father glowered at me. "You, I know you're behind it all."

Mother grabbed his arm. "What's going on?"

Father took several deep breaths as he attempted to calm down. "Old Bing came by. He wanted to repay me the money he borrowed. He's the one who told me. Our boys went all over Chinatown begging for food."

Mother put a hand to her mouth. "They had all these bags."

Father groaned. "We're the laughingstock of Chinatown." When Mother began to laugh, he glared at her. "I don't see what's so funny."

"You told them to get leftovers," Mother said.

After a moment, Father sighed reluctantly. "I guess I did."

"And at least you got Old Bing to pay up," Mother pointed out.

"I thought I'd kissed that money good-bye," Father agreed.

"I'm sorry, Father," I apologized. "We told them it was for our alligator."

"They thought it was an excuse," Father explained. "They thought it really was for you and you were just trying to save your pride."

"What if we borrow Uncle Curtis's camera. Then you can take a picture and show it to your friends and prove it was for Oscar."

"A man carries around a picture of his kids, not their pet alligator." He relented. "But I guess I'll have to. I'll borrow a camera tomorrow." He glared at me. "I'll show it around as Teddy's nuttiest idea."

At that moment, the doorbell began ringing furiously. Bobby must have got it because the next moment I heard his voice along with that of Mr. Wong, our landlord. Mr. Wong gave one of his familiar coughs, and then his voice floated through the apartment. "Don't hide, Blessed Strength. I saw you sneak home. How many times do I have to tell you: all you renters have to use the one trash can. The other's mine."

Puzzled, Father turned to Mother. She gave another chuckle. "I told the boys to throw away the garbage."

"There were lots of bags, Father," I told him.

Mr. Wong got so mad, he forgot to cough. Instead, he shouted even louder from the doorway. "You can't throw your trash from the store into my can. It's filled with scraps."

"They're scraps of meat, not fish," I tried to explain.

Mr. Wong was so worked up that he didn't hear me. "I've got a good mind to dump it all in your kitchen."

"You and your presents," Father groaned. "I wish I'd never heard of alligators."

At this point, I thought it was better to go back to the Council of Trent. I began writing diligently while Father and Mother went off to apologize.

chapter fifteen

Father stayed home rather than going back to reopen the store. That wasn't like him at all. He kept the store open from morning to night. The only day he closed was Christmas. When he didn't reopen the store, I knew he was really embarrassed. He was scared of meeting another club member. He just sat in the living room staring at our television.

I felt so bad that I went over to him. "I'm sorry, Father. I should never have gotten Oscar. I didn't mean to hurt your pride."

"It's not just my pride," he said. "It's all of ours."

Glancing at the television, I saw something was wrong with the vertical hold. The picture kept flipping past like a broken movie film. "I'll go over and borrow the camera tonight. Then you can have a photograph to prove your crazy son bought an alligator."

Father heaved himself up in the chair. "You're not crazy. You just don't think."

"Yes, sir," I said, still feeling miserable.

He squirmed uncomfortably in his seat. "If you could apply your mind, there's no telling what you could do."

It was the first time I'd ever heard praise from him. "Really?"

He tapped his fingers on the chair arms as if pondering something. "White parents flatter their kids so they get swelled heads. Chinese parents are smarter. They may not say anything to their kids, but that doesn't mean they're not proud of them."

"I'll try," I promised.

"Maybe it wouldn't hurt every now and then, though." He surprised me by putting his arms around me and squeezing. But as soon as we heard Mother's footsteps, he pushed me away. With a wink, he put a fingertip to his lips.

As it turned out, I didn't have to visit Uncle Curtis to get his camera because he and Aunt Ethel came to us. We were just finishing dinner when we heard the doorbell.

"We were just having dinner." I said as I led them into the dining room.

"We were too tired to cook tonight so we ate out," said Aunt Ethel, "and we had some extra. We thought you could use this." Uncle Curtis held up a doggy bag.

Father frowned when he saw it. "We don't need charity," he said.

Uncle Curtis pulled it back. "It's not for you, Harold."

Father was annoyed. "My kids eat what I eat and I eat what my kids eat."

Uncle Curtis shrugged. "It's for the pet."

"You bring gifts of food for an alligator?" Father demanded.

Uncle Curtis stared at Father. "I don't want my nephews collecting garbage."

The doorbell rang. When I answered it, I saw it was Uncle Mat. He and Aunt Martha had a doggy bag, too.

Grandmother brought a whole shopping bag filled with a dozen cartons. "I had lunch with my friends," she explained.

We had so many relatives there, it seemed like another party.

"I give up," Father said, and held up his hands. "Curtis, I need your camera tomorrow."

"I'll bring it by on the way to the office," Uncle Curtis promised.

Father nodded his thanks and then turned to Bobby. "I've learned my lesson. There are worse things than wasting food. You can have day-old fish. Okay?"

Bobby picked up the nearest doggy bag from the pile on the table. "You and Mother are the only ones who haven't fed Oscar."

"I'll pass," Mother said quickly.

Bobby turned to Father. "Would you like to give him a snack?"

Father sighed. "Why not?"

Uncle Mat hunted around in the pile until he found his doggy bag. "Take mine. I made sure that I had some spareribs."

Father leaned away from Uncle Mat. "You picked your meal so you could feed tidbits to an alligator?"

Uncle Mat's face grew red. "I would have eaten spareribs anyway."

Uncle Curtis wormed his doggy bag from the bottom of the pile. "He could choke on a bone. Use mine, not Mat's."

Uncle Mat blocked Uncle Curtis. "You think you're so smart. Alligators eat whole people. So what's a little rib bone?"

"This is a little alligator." Uncle Mat reached around Uncle Curtis and dangled his bag at Father. "This is soft."

Father glanced in it after he took it. "This is chopped eggplant. Alligators aren't vegetarians."

Uncle Mat laughed. "The cheapskate finished all the meat."

"Enough," Grandmother announced, and the three men fell silent. "I've got barbecued pork somewhere in my bag."

When we had found the right carton, we all trooped down the hallway to the bathroom. Bobby was the first to enter. "It's gone."

Father was next in line. "What do you mean, gone?"

Bobby began hunting around the bathroom. "It's not in the pan, and it's not in the tub."

Everyone looked down at their feet at the same instant—just in case Oscar was about to snip off a toe. We helped Bobby search the bathroom, but there was no sign of his pet.

"It was so thin, it could hide anywhere," Aunt Martha said. She kept her eyes on the floor for some sign of Oscar.

Like Aunt Martha, Uncle Curtis was afraid to take his eyes off the floor. "It'll come out when it's hungry."

Father was also reluctant to look up. "Uh, Curtis, can alligators climb?"

Uncle Curtis plucked his lip. "Well, I did some reading, and there are some reports that they can rear up on their hind legs."

Still keeping an eye out for Oscar, Father asked, "So how high is that?"

Uncle Curtis placed his flat palm parallel to the floor. "I'd say about that high."

Father was relieved. "Good. They can't climb up on the beds."

Mother didn't dare raise her head either, even when she was being practical. "Does anyone want a snack? I'll heat up the other doggy bags."

"Maybe the smell of food will draw out Oscar," Uncle Mat suggested.

While poor Bobby continued his search, we walked on tiptoe back into the dining room.

As Mother warmed the leftovers, the smell gradually filled the apartment. Mother kept me near her as a lookout just in case Oscar tried a sneak attack. Once Mother had served the leftovers, it turned into the funniest meal I ever had. Everyone's head was bowed because they were looking for Oscar. Everyone also put their feet up on the chair legs to make it harder for Oscar to snack on them.

No one seemed to have an appetite anyway. It was still too close to dinner. Besides, we were too busy waiting for Oscar to join us.

As soon as it was polite, everyone left. "Still want me to bring the camera?" Uncle Curtis asked.

"Yes. He'll turn up," Father said resignedly.

"I hope no one flushed him into the sewer." Uncle Mat laughed.

"That's impossible," Uncle Curtis insisted.

"And it isn't appreciated." Mother nodded in the direction of the bathroom where Bobby still was.

The really funny thing was that no one used the bathroom that evening, not even Grandmother. Just in case Uncle Mat was right about Oscar.

chapter sixteen

As I helped Mother squeeze the leftovers into our already crammed refrigerator, she looked at me. "Why did you help Bobby anyway?"

As I handed her a carton, I tried to pass it off with a shrug. "He would have messed up. And that would have ruined our reputation, too."

To my surprise, she gave me a quick peck on the cheek. "You're so much like your father. You can't admit to doing a good deed, can you?"

I rubbed the wet spot on my cheek. "I am?"

Mother laughed. "He was a regular little devil when he was your age."

"What kind of things did he do?" I wondered.

Mother, though, brought a finger to her lips as we heard Father come into the kitchen.

"Honey," he asked, "are there any spareribs left?"

Mother winked. We had our own secret now. "Yes, but let me heat them up. You'll get sick if you eat them cold." She started to dig around in the refrigerator again.

When I had finished helping Mother, I went into the bathroom. Bobby was still there searching for Oscar. He was on his hands and knees, peering at the cracks in a tiled wall.

"It's time to go to bed." I pulled at his shoulder. "Come on. Get up."

Instead of rising, he looked over his shoulder at me. "I can't go to bed until I find Oscar."

I could see tear tracks on his cheeks, and that was unusual. Even when I was tormenting Bobby at my worst, he never cried. "Oscar will turn up."

He just stayed where he was. "You're not mad, are you?"

Surprised, I sat down on the edge of the bathtub. "Why would you think that?"

"You gave him to me. Oscar was special, and I lost him," Bobby said.

I could feel my cheeks begin to burn a bright red. "He wasn't *that* special."

Bobby pulled himself up beside me. "Everyone made such a fuss at the party. It was better than any toy."

I got some tissues from the box on top of the toilet tank. "I have a confession," I said. "I was playing a trick on you when I gave you Oscar."

He took the tissue and wiped his eyes. "I wondered about that."

I felt like squirming. "It was just a little prank, though. Like grabbing a chair out from under you."

"How would you like it if I did that to you?" he asked.

I thought back to his pet's christening. "Isn't that why you wanted to name it Teddy at first?"

"Kind of," he admitted reluctantly. "But I didn't care. I told you how I liked alligators. It was like having my own nature show."

The kid had more character than I had thought. (Okay, his older brother was too dense to realize Bobby had been playing his own prank.) I began to feel the first glimmerings of respect for my little brother. "The joke's on me, anyway."

I had never seen Bobby so worried before. He used the tissue until it was a damp lump. "The joke's on poor Oscar. I bet he's hiding somewhere, scared and lost."

I'd done stuff to Bobby as long as I had known him. That's what older brothers are for. (If it was up to our folks, they would have spoiled him shamelessly.) Up until now, though, Bobby had always been like a helium balloon. Even when I had tried to yank down on his string, I could feel his spirits tugging to go back up. It used to drive me crazy. Just once I wish he could have acted normal like everyone else.

But even at my worst, I had never wanted him to feel this low. I pulled more tissues from the box and handed them to him. "Nothing scares an animal with that many teeth."

He blew his nose. "But he trusted me to protect him."

The only thing Oscar wanted was three square meals a day. However, you don't kick someone when they're down so I kept my opinion to myself. That was a first for Gator Boy.

Somehow, though, that didn't seem enough. While Bobby snuffled miserably, I sat uncomfortably, wondering what to do. Finally, I figured that alligators—and gator boys—must be nice to their own.

So I put my arm around Bobby. I did it kind of clumsily. It wasn't as if I'd had a lot of practice. "And where could he get lost in our apartment?"

He blew his nose even louder. "He could squeeze through some hole in the wall."

I imagined Oscar poking his head out of a mouse hole. "We won't have to worry about mice anymore, then."

"He could get stuck, though," Bobby said.

I tried to reassure him. "We'd hear him wriggling around if he was. Then I'd borrow Father's hammer, and we'd knock a hole in that old wall and get him out."

"You would?" Bobby rubbed the back of his hand across his eyes.

I looked down at him. Right now he didn't seem so obnoxious.

"Scout's honor," I said. To my own surprise, I meant it. "Now let's go to bed." He got up when I pulled at him.

Things still weren't the same the next day. When I got up in the morning, I picked up my slippers and started to put them on. Something, though, made me stop. I shook out first one and then the other.

Bobby had been watching. "Oscar's too big to fit in them," he said.

I had left my corduroy pants on the floor. When I picked them up, I shook them out cautiously and laid them on the bed. I saw Bobby do the same. At least for a while, we wouldn't be dumping our clothes on the floor.

Mother was in the kitchen walking around on tiptoe. She looked ready to bolt at the first sign of something green. Her mind was so taken up with Oscar that everything came out burned or undercooked.

Father ate breakfast with his feet propped up on a big, red hundred-pound rice can. He wanted them out of reach of alligators, too.

I had had time to think about things overnight. The situation called for something more than a photograph. "I'm sorry about our good name," I apologized again. "Would it help if I went around to your friends?"

Father picked up a forkful of runny scrambled eggs over undercooked rice. "It's okay. I'll handle them."

I had placed my chair away from the table so I could see anything sneaking up on me. This meant I had to lean far forward to eat. "But you can't photograph Oscar now."

Father grinned at Mother. I guess he'd been thinking about things last night, too. "We've got an anniversary coming up. Maybe we'll hold a big banquet. We'll show everyone we're not poor."

"That would be nice," Mother said uncertainly as she sat down with us. "But can we afford it?"

Father shrugged. "Big shot Curtis is always bragging about his connections at that fancy restaurant. We'll see if he really can get us a good deal."

After school was over, I looked for Bobby but I didn't see him. Then I saw one of his classmates at the bus stop—I couldn't remember the little twerp's name. "Have you seen Bobby?" I asked.

He pointed up the steep Clay Street hill. "He already left. I think he was going home."

I glanced up the hill, but there wasn't any sign of him. "But we have Chinese school next."

"He's cutting it, I guess," the classmate said.

That wasn't like Bobby either. I was the one who was always trying to get out of Chinese school. Bobby took it so he could understand Grandmother better. (The funny thing was that they taught us a different dialect in school, so Grandmother didn't always understand him anyway.)

I headed up the hill. When I got home, I found Bobby in the hallway. He had his ear against the wall while he rapped it with his knuckle. "Oscar," he called. "Oscar."

He was so upset that I did not try to scold him. "He's not hiding in the walls, Bobby. He's probably curled up behind some chair."

"Will you help me search?" he begged.

He looked so sad that I could not argue. "Sure," I said.

We'd still had no luck when Mother came home from work. She understood when I explained why we had cut class, and she promised to write a note to the Chinese school principal.

In the meantime, she got a plate from the kitchen and put some leftovers on it. "Oscar's got to be hungry by now," she said.

For the next few days, we set out little plates of Oscar tidbits to tempt him. Every night, Father counted the guppies in his aquarium, but none were missing. Maybe Oscar was eating mice after all.

chapter seventeen

It's funny how you learn to adjust. It got to be second nature to inspect everything before I sat down. When I walked in our apartment, I kept one eye out for an alligator tail—or worse, the sharper end.

As Oscar stayed lost day after day, I began to think he was D-E-A-D. From the way they had begun to relax, I knew Mother and Father thought the same thing. Even so, none of us said anything in front of Bobby.

It was crazy, I know. Maybe in the old days before Oscar I would have, but as dopey as Bobby could be, I wanted to protect him.

Bobby never gave up hope. His faith acted like a kind of shield. Facts just bounced off his faith.

Then, late one afternoon, we were walking up the hill after Chinese school when we saw our landlord, Mr. Wong, crossing Powell. He must have been shopping in Chinatown because he had a bag in either hand. At the top of one bag, I could see some sort of new herbal cure.

As always, he wore his blue suit with the white pin-stripes. Every now and then he gave one of his dry little coughs.

In the bed beneath the cable car tracks, the cable hummed and clattered as it moved. I stopped to look both ways, but a desperate Bobby shot across the street. Fortunately there wasn't any traffic, and I darted after him.

Bobby, though, had already caught up with our landlord. "Mr. Wong," he called. "Wait, Mr. Wong. Have you heard something in the walls?"

Usually our landlord did his best to avoid us. I think he was afraid we would ask him to fix one of the many problems with our apartment. If he couldn't hide from us, he tried to ignore us.

He kept his eyes stonily on the sidewalk while Bobby kept pace beside him. "Mr. Wong, have you heard something slither in the walls?"

Even Mr. Wong could not neglect that. He stopped dead in his tracks, his shopping bags banging against his legs. "Slither?"

"Like an alligator?" Bobby asked hopefully.

Mr. Wong hawked and spat on the sidewalk. "Haven't you found that thing yet?"

"No," Bobby puffed, "and I thought he might have got into the walls and gone downstairs."

Alarmed, Mr. Wong cried, "Into my apartment?" his voice rising an octave.

I dashed up the last few yards. "Don't worry, Mr. Wong," I panted. "Bobby's just being overanxious."

"Sure." Mr. Wong laughed nervously.

Bobby defended himself. "Well, what other possibility is there? We've looked all over the apartment. He must be eating something."

"In our apartment." I emphasized the *our.* "Alligators don't get into walls."

"Sure," Mr. Wong said, but he didn't laugh this time. In fact, I think we had scared his cough right out of him. He took a step forward and then hesitated. "Better to be safe than sorry," Mr. Wong muttered. Turning on his heel, he checked that the street was clear of cars and plunged across.

On the other side of the street was an exterminator. A big sign over his store said THE REINCARNATOR. SEND THAT VERMIN ON TO ANOTHER LIFE. I knew him from Father's club. It was hard to tell when he was serious and when he was joking.

"Now see what you've done," I accused Bobby. Making sure that there were no cars in the street, I hurried after Mr. Wong. I could hear Bobby at my heels.

The Reincarnator was a small, thin man with a pale, narrow face. He always wore gray coveralls and a cap. He was just putting down the phone and reached over the countertop to drag a pad in front of him. "What's the problem, friend?"

Mr. Wong smiled apologetically. "I don't really know how to begin."

The Reincarnator finished writing out a bill. "It's no shame to have mice and cockroaches. Vermin like to sneak into the houses of decent people. If you have a problem, sing out loud."

Embarrassed, Mr. Wong leaned forward. "How would I check my walls for alligators?"

The Reincarnator calmly laid his pen down. Folding up the bill, he stuffed it into an envelope. "Well, you got to set up an alligator trap."

Mr. Wong drew his eyebrows together while he puzzled that out. "And how do I do that?"

The Reincarnator licked the envelope and sealed it by pounding his fist. "You have to catch a live mouse. Then you take a string and tie it to the leg of a chair and hide. If you've got alligators in the wall, they'll smell the mouse and come out."

"Really?" Mr. Wong asked doubtfully.

"It works every time, friend." The Reincarnator tore a stamp from a roll.

Mr. Wong studied the Reincarnator's face, but he seemed perfectly serious. "And . . . and what do I do then?"

The Reincarnator licked the stamp and thumped it

onto the envelope with his fist. "How big are these alligators?"

Mr. Wong turned as we joined him at the counter. "What's the size?"

Bobby held up his hands in the approximate length of Oscar.

The Reincarnator dumped the envelope on top of a pile of other envelopes in a wire basket. "Have you got a twenty-two?"

"No!" Bobby said in horror. "You can't shoot it." He would have tugged at Mr. Wong, but I wrapped my arms around my brother's shoulders.

"You wouldn't happen to have a spare mouse in some trap?" Even now, he was trying to save a buck.

With a smirk, the Reincarnator picked up his pen and clicked it shut. Then with a flick of his wrist, he slid it into his plastic shirt-pocket protector like some swordsman sheathing his weapon. "Fat Man put you up to this, didn't he? You tell him this practical joke didn't work."

Mr. Wong tried to shrug sheepishly, but his shopping bags weighed his shoulders down. "This is no prank. We really have alligators. Just ask them."

I had to get Bobby out of there before anyone said the *d*-word. "It's only one alligator," I said. "It's just hiding somewhere in our apartment."

The Reincarnator nodded slowly. "You're that crazy boy of Blessed Strength's. So there really is an alligator." He rested his elbows on the countertop. "What did you do? Flush it into the sewer?"

"I didn't do anything," I said indignantly.

The Reincarnator leaned against the counter and studied the ceiling as if there were instructions printed there. "I'm making an educated guess, but it comes free. If you haven't seen your alligator by now, he's dead."

I took in my breath sharply. He had said the dreaded word.

It was awful to see Bobby's face. He looked as if the Reincarnator had just cut off one of his ears.

"He's not dead," Bobby insisted.

The Reincarnator looked down. "Have it your way, boy. Your walls are full of alligators. Good luck getting rid of them."

"He's not dead!" Bobby shouted, and ran from the store.

chapter eighteen

Even though Bobby had a head start, he could not get very far ahead of me. The hill was just too steep.

When I left the store, I saw him twenty feet away. The slanting sidewalk had reduced his run to a walk. I called to him, but he kept puffing along like a small locomotive.

I didn't try to run after him up that steep hill, but I tried not to let the distance between us increase. Even so, he set a pretty hard pace.

When we were within sight of our apartment, I put on a burst and caught up with him. It wasn't that I was faster. My legs were just longer.

"Bobby," I panted.

"Shut up," he snapped.

"That guy didn't know what he was saying," I panted.

"He makes his living killing things," Bobby said. I

could hear the hurt in his voice, and I wanted to protect him.

"He just kills bugs and mice—not tough old alligators." I sat down on our steps to get my breath back.

Bobby wanted an excuse to hope. "Do you really think so?" he asked as he stood in front of me.

I was glad I had fibbed. "Sure." I slapped his leg. "Tell you what. I'll check the bathroom while you check the bedroom this time. Okay?"

He smiled like the old Bobby. "Thanks."

I got out my keys. I know it sounds silly, but it was the first time I had ever felt like we were kin. "You're my brother. What do you expect?"

I was so busy pondering my newfound feelings that I dropped my bag on the steps. Then I took off my coat and left that on the stairs. As I stood before the bathroom, I saw that Bobby was carrying my things.

"We've got enough people shouting at us," he explained as he headed into our bedroom. "Besides, what if Oscar got into them?"

I shook my head. People were bound to like Bobby better than me, but he worked at it. He treated it like his job in life. It was too much work for me. Well, who needs lots of friends? Your hand gets worn out writing all those Christmas cards.

Feeling better, I went into the bathroom to look for signs of Oscar.

I never expected to find Oscar himself. So at first I thought it was a stick on the bathroom floor. Then I saw the little legs protruding from either side. Oscar was just lying there on his belly.

Hoping he was asleep, I whispered, "Oscar." I got ready to jump back if he lifted his snout, but the alligator didn't move.

That wasn't a good sign at all. I edged closer and nudged him with my toe. When he remained still, I risked bending over.

Oscar was dead—maybe from a lack of water. In fact, he looked just like one of those dried-out victims in a desert. His snout was aimed toward the toilet bowl. I guess that was his target.

I wanted to check for a pulse, but I wasn't sure where to look. I tried around the neck, but the hide was cold and stiff. Oscar was definitely dead.

Suddenly I remembered my last conversation with Bobby. I had great timing to promise that Oscar was alive. I couldn't break Bobby's heart. I got a pink towel and wrapped it around Oscar. With a little luck, I could sneak Oscar down to the trash can while he was in the bedroom.

Bobby, though, heard me. "Have you had any luck?" he asked.

"No," I said. I tried to keep myself between him and the towel. "Well, I'd better get some chores done. I promised to hang this up to dry."

Bobby came down the hallway. "You never help us with the laundry."

I tried to back away. "I thought I ought to. I mean, everybody's been so upset."

"What's in the towel?" Bobby asked.

I was in an even worse jam. "I wasn't trying to play any trick," I said.

"It's Oscar, isn't it?" Bobby asked.

"I shouldn't have shot off my mouth without know-ing," I said.

Bobby stopped near me. "Let me see," he insisted.

I unwrapped the towel. Oscar was stiff—as if he had been starched. "I'm sorry, Bobby."

Bobby stared at Oscar. "You weren't going to just dump him into the garbage can, were you?"

I tried to avoid that question since that had been my exact intention. "I'll save up and get you another," I promised.

Bobby covered his pet with the towel again. "It's okay. One was enough."

"You sure?" I asked.

"An alligator's neat, but they get everyone else too ex-cited," Bobby decided.

I was feeling a little stupid standing there with a dead alligator. "What should we do with him, then? We could go to that taxidermist. He stuffed that trout Aunt Norma caught."

"I don't want to put Oscar up on a wall." He took the

alligator from me and knelt. "Oscar should have a funeral."

"Where?" I asked. Chinatown is all asphalt and brick and concrete. "The only patch of grass is that lawn behind the projects."

"There's that little park up on Nob Hill," Bobby suggested.

"Across from the cathedral?" I asked. "You're crazy."

"I'll do it by myself then." He petted Oscar in a way that Oscar would never have allowed when he was alive.

Bobby was much worse than he had been when Oscar was lost. Then, he had just been feeling sad. Now, he was actually mourning his alligator.

The weird part was this: seeing Bobby in pain made me hurt inside, too. Whether I liked it or not, there was a bond between us. For the second time that day, I felt like I really had a brother.

"I'm sorry," I said.

He didn't look up as he cradled his dead pet. "It's not your fault."

As I watched him grieve, I thought, Yes, it is. If I hadn't given it to you, you wouldn't be hurting now.

Bobby got up and started for the steps. "I'll be back soon."

I drew my eyebrows together. "You can't do it now."

Bobby turned sideways. "I figured I wouldn't upset Mother or Father anymore."

I shook my head. "Do you really have to bury him up at that park?"

"It's nice up there with the fountain and the pigeons," Bobby explained. "Oscar would like it."

I thought to myself, The only thing Oscar would have liked is biting off some pigeon's head. However, I didn't say that idea out loud.

What could I do? As much as it might pain me to admit it, he was my brother, warts and all. Don't make any mistake. I was not getting mushy. But brothers had to stick together. With a sigh, I said, "We'll have to wait until it's dark."

"You'll think up some excuse for us," Bobby said gratefully. Then he licked his lips as he began to figure out the operation. "We'll need something to put Oscar in so Mother and Father won't suspect."

He spoke as if he were planning the invasion of Normandy. Feeling silly, I suggested, "I'll get Father's duffel bag."

Bobby nodded, "And we'll need something to dig with."

Bobby may not have been that imaginative, but he was thorough. I had to admire that. "Get a couple of Mother's big cooking spoons," I said.

"Right." As I headed for our parents' bedroom, he started for the kitchen. With his dead pet still in his arms, he suddenly stopped and turned. "Thanks, Teddy."

For some strange reason, I didn't feel nearly as foolish now. "Forget it," I said. "What are brothers for?"

chapter nineteen

Father gave us a scare when he came home early at
eight-thirty and took a bath. He emerged in his old
plaid wool bathrobe. His damp hair stuck up in spikes.
Around his neck was the pink towel I had tried to use
to hide Oscar from Bobby. I had refolded it and put it
in the pile of clean towels.

"Honey," he called to Mother. "This towel smells
funny. Did you change soap?"

"No, it should be the same as always," Mother called
from the kitchen.

Father sniffed one end. "But it smells like . . .
like . . ." I sat on the couch, waiting for him to say "alligator." However, Father had not been around Oscar
enough to place the smell. "Like old mud," Father finished.

"Well, put it in the hamper and get a clean one,"
Mother snapped.

"It's okay." Father calmly began to use the left side of

the towel to dry his hair. His face was hidden by the towel.

"Father?" I asked. "Can we go over to the Chinese Rec Center and shoot some baskets? It's Friday." The Chinese Rec Center was a gymnasium near the cable car museum. My words weren't exactly a fib. Bobby and I would stop by there after the funeral and shoot some token baskets.

A corner of the towel rose to reveal an eye. "Did you do your homework?"

I knew our parents would ask that particular question, so Bobby and I had been diligent about finishing our school assignments. "Yes."

"Did you ask your mother?" He went on toweling himself vigorously.

"Yes, she said it was okay as long as you agreed," I said.

He gave a grunt. "Be back by ten," he said. As he passed by, I caught a very faint whiff of dead alligator. I hoped Mother washed the clothes really well or we might have something to remember Oscar by.

When we sat down to dinner, Mother used soup spoons to serve things. "I can't find my big kitchen spoons," she said. "Have you seen them, Teddy?"

"No, I'm sorry," I answered truthfully. When anything was missing, Mother always asked me, never Bobby. That's why I had Bobby "borrow" them.

Unfortunately Bobby's conscience couldn't rest. As

Mother served dinner with her improvised spoons, he asked, "Can Mr. Wong make us leave because of Oscar?"

I kicked him under the table. I didn't want him bringing up our last conversation with our landlord.

Father took his plate from Mother. "Of course not. The apartments belong to his wife, and she's one of Grandmother's friends. They play mah-jongg all the time."

"Better tell Grandmother to let her win," I suggested, half in earnest.

"You tell your grandmother," Father said. When it came to mah-jongg, Grandmother showed no mercy, even to her grandchildren.

As Bobby and I ate quickly, Father joked. "Are you sure you're just going to shoot baskets? Are there going to be some girls there, too?"

"Harold, they're too young," Mother scolded.

"I was Teddy's age when I first noticed you," Father laughed. "You were this skinny little girl who could make a basket from anywhere on the court." He pantomimed shooting a basketball. "Swoosh. Swoosh."

"That didn't keep you from tripping me," Mother said, but she was smiling.

While they reminisced, I wolfed the rest of my food down. I didn't want them asking any more incriminating questions. And I didn't want to leave Bobby's conscience more time to work.

Bobby had already cleaned his plate like a human vacuum cleaner and was waiting for me. At a nod, we both got up. From our bedroom closet, I took the duffel bag that held the late Oscar. Inside, I could hear the two big kitchen spoons rattling.

"Wait," Bobby said. He had made a little cross out of Popsicle sticks and Scotch tape. When he unzipped the bag to put it in, I caught a whiff of Oscar. Bobby's pet was beginning to turn. I'd definitely have to air out the bag afterward.

chapter twenty

Outside it was a clear, crisp night. The city, with all its twinkling lights, dipped sharply toward the bay. The waters were like ink except where they picked up the lights of the land and the sky. Upon the rolling surface of the bay, the reflections of the stars and the street lamps seemed to dance together. The Bay Bridge was a black silhouette, flat as a paper cutout. At the very top of the towers, red lights winked like thumbtacks pinning it to the night sky. Across the bay, Oakland glittered like a golden necklace wrapped around the throats of the dark hills.

At Mason Street we turned left. Rising into the sky, we could see the tower of the Fairmont Hotel. It soared over the hill like a massive-shouldered giant. The track of the outside elevator was a broad white column that glowed as it zipped up toward the rotating restaurant above. The tower's lights were so bright that they obscured the stars overhead.

We turned up Sacramento Street, which slanted even more sharply. We could see the rest of the hotel, filling the rest of the block.

Uncle Mat played trombone in the Fairmont's Venetian Room. He was always bringing us all sorts of neat little toys that got served with the drinks and snacks: flags of various countries, tiny paper parasols, or plastic cutlasses. He pulled them out of his pockets as if his supply would never end.

At the top of the hill, we paused long enough to get our breath. A white stretch limousine rolled through the ornate gate and up the hotel's driveway. When it stopped, the driver jumped out. He was in a black suit and bow tie, but he had a little peaked cap on his head. He opened the door for a woman in furs and a man in a tuxedo. As the uniformed doorman opened the door with a bow, from somewhere deep inside the hotel I thought I heard Uncle Mat's trombone calling, bright and sassy.

Across the street was a big Victorian mansion, and beyond that was Huntington Square. Past its hedges rose the spires of Grace Cathedral.

We crossed the street and circled the mansion to the other side where there was a little park bordered by a high hedge. The fountain was still splashing in the middle of the park though there wasn't a pigeon in sight.

"This way," Bobby whispered. Crouching, we ran like two commandos across the square toward a wooden bench.

Apparently, Bobby had already picked out the spot. We slid between the bench and the hedge. Bobby pointed to a place in the dirt between two big roots of a hedge. "Here." He knelt by a spot.

I set down the duffel bag and took a breath before I unzipped it. I didn't want to smell the concentrated perfume of the late Oscar. Fishing out both spoons, I handed one to Bobby. "Make it deep," I said, and got down on my knees beside him. I used my free hand to hold the branches up so we would have room to work.

Together we plunged our spoons into the soft dirt at the roots of the hedge. We piled up the dirt to the side. In the dark beneath the hedge, it was a little hard to be sure the hole was big enough. When I judged we had taken out enough dirt, I said, "Let's try to put Oscar in."

"Okay." Bobby set his spoon down and reverently took Oscar out of the bag.

I knelt with the spoon on my knee as Bobby leaned forward. His arms disappeared under the hedge as he placed his dead pet into the hole. "It's a good fit," he informed me.

I started to put the dirt into the hole with a spoon, but Bobby didn't even bother with one. Instead, he shoved his pile of earth with the flats of his palms. Once the hole was full, I tamped it down with my spoon.

When I turned around, Bobby had his grave marker in one hand and a handful of flowers in the other.

"Where'd you get the flowers from?" I asked. All the florists were closed, and there were no parks that had flowers around here.

"From Mrs. Wong's window box in the back," Bobby said. "You can just reach it from the rear staircase."

As Bobby set the cross in the dirt and decorated it with flowers, I picked up the spoons. I shook off as much dirt as I could before I put them back into the bag. "You'd better hope she doesn't notice."

"Maybe Grandmother will have a streak of bad luck and Mrs. Wong will win for a change." Bobby sat back on his heels.

The whole evening had begun to feel like an adventure. No doubt, tomorrow I'd feel silly all over again, but at that instant I was caught up in the moment. "Do you want to say anything?" I asked.

"Why?" Bobby demanded.

"It's customary at funerals," I said.

"Not this time." He raised his head and looked above the hedge at the big stained-glass windows of the cathedral. There must have been some kind of service. The inner lights made the windows burn with sharp intensity. I heard an organ playing something solemn and yet sweet.

On the other side of the hedge, the California Street cable car clanged its bell as it rolled by. Its notes floated upward, merging with the organ music. As the fountain splashed merrily behind us, I found myself mumbling, "I wouldn't mind being buried here either."

From somewhere nearby I heard the sound of many voices. Through a gap in the hedge, I could see across California Street. There must have been some kind of concert in the temple because dressed-up people were spilling down its steps and out onto the sidewalk.

"We'd better go," I said, and got up.

It was just as well that we had finished when we did. A man in a pea coat came into the square. In one gloved hand, he held the leash of a dog. The man looked as bored as the dog looked excited. Friskily it darted this way and that, tugging at the leash.

We were starting out of the park when Bobby looked over his shoulder and froze. We saw the dog sniffing around the bench where we had just been. Pivoting, Bobby was going to defend his pet.

I put my hand on his shoulder and dragged him back. "We can't do anything," I whispered fiercely.

"But it's not right," Bobby protested as the dog slid behind the bench. "Not on Oscar's first night here." He twisted his head toward the man. "Hey, mister!"

The man glanced toward us. "Yes?"

"Bobby, no," I whispered. "He'll tell the gardeners, and they'll just dig up Oscar. And then we'll have to do this all over again."

The man was watching us and not his pet. Helpless, we saw it approach Oscar's grave. When it caught a whiff of dead alligator, the startled dog leaped backward like some furry flea.

"What's gotten into you, boy?" the man said to his pet.

However, the little dog simply stood by his legs as it began barking frantically.

Oscar had its own defenses, I guess. Its lingering scent was better than any alligator jaws. "Never mind," I said.

We left him still trying to quiet his dog.

chapter twenty-one

On the way home we stopped by the Chinese Rec Center. I shot a basket and then handed the ball to Bobby. He raised it over one shoulder and launched it toward the basket. He missed even the backboard, but the truth was served. "Close enough," I said. "Let's go home."

When we got back, though, Mother called me into the dining room. I was afraid someone had spotted us, but Father shoved a sheet of binder paper over the tabletop toward me. "Read this."

In Mother's neat handwriting, I read:

I, the undersigned, promise never to buy anything
  1. with teeth and claws
  2. sharp
  3. flammable
  4. poisonous

5. explosive

6. contagious.

When I looked up, Mother asked, "Do you understand it?"

"I guess so," I said.

"Yes or no?" Father demanded.

When I nodded, Mother set a pen down in front of me. "Sign it," she said.

My parents were trying to hem me in. There wasn't a lot of room for the imagination. "If I sign this, all I can ever buy for a present is socks."

"Fine," Father said. "Sign. We want to survive your imagination until you grow up and move out."

However, I thought I could smell a deal. Normally, Father expected us to live within our allowance—as long as we did our chores. Instead of taking the pen, I got up and went around the table. I stood between my parents and whispered, "Can you lend me some money? I want to buy another present for Bobby."

Father jingled the coins in his pocket nervously. "What kind of present?" he whispered back. "Socks, I hope."

I kept my voice low. "A turtle."

He eyed me suspiciously. "How big a turtle?"

"About three inches long," I said softly. "So the claws won't be very big."

He didn't have much faith in me. "How big does it grow?"

"I don't know," I shrugged, "but you can probably outrun it."

Father and Mother laughed—a bit harder than necessary. "Except when you're buying presents, you're a good boy," Mother said.

I looked at her in surprise. "Thank you."

"Don't get a swelled head now," Father warned, but he was smiling.

"No, sir," I promised.

"You can help me out in the store next Saturday." He handed me some money.

I folded the bill up and pocketed it. Then I went around the table and signed the pledge with a flourish.

"I'll pick up another turtle home," Mother promised.

As we walked back down the hallway, Bobby whispered, "I didn't think you'd give in that easy."

I put my arm around his shoulder and patted him. "It'll be a challenge, but that's what imaginations are for."

Bobby was bubbling with curiosity. "What did you tell them? Why did they give you money?"

"So you want answers?" I asked. When Bobby jerked his head up and down, I chuckled. "That's what imaginations are for," I repeated.

The next day I took the money downtown and

bought a turtle. Bobby loved it. He named it Bertle the Turtle.

What can I say? Bobby likes dumb, cute names. Even so, he's still my brother. I really know that now. You have a brother when out of the whole wide world only you two share a secret. We have a tiny grave and cross up in a fancy park that's meant for rich folks. No one else knows—except maybe for you now.

Perhaps the park gardeners know, too. Every now and then Bobby comes up the back stairs with a few flowers. He puts them into a paper bag and leaves the house. I figure he takes them from Mrs. Wong's window box. If she notices, she doesn't say anything. I also assume that he brings them up to that little grave. If the gardeners notice, they don't say anything either. After all, Oscar can't hurt the pigeons now.

Otherwise, things returned to normal. My parents made a point of apologizing formally to our landlady, Mrs. Wong. Reassured by my written pledge, she forgave us all. She even laughed about it. "Teddy will do great things," she predicted, and added, "if someone doesn't shoot him first."

She and my parents stopped worrying about Oscar after a while. Everyone figured he had crawled out of the house somehow and down to the bay—or rather, almost everyone thought that. There was one exception.

Every now and then we'd hear a soft tapping from

below. For a long time, I didn't know what it was. If Mr. Wong was putting up pictures, he had an awful lot of them.

It was only months later that we found out. Grandmother had played mah-jongg with our landlady, Mrs. Wong. Giggling, Grandmother told us over the telephone that Mr. Wong was still checking for alligators. Mrs. Wong couldn't make him stop.

I asked Grandmother to ask Mrs. Wong if he was tying a live mouse to the leg of a chair. But I couldn't make Grandmother understand—either in Chinese or English.

I never did find out.

afterword

Now that alligators have been listed as an endangered species at different times, I know it was wrong to buy one. Certainly one should not purchase any pet without the proper equipment and knowledge. When I was a boy, I can only say that most people gave little thought to the comfort and safety of animals. Many little turtles had their shells painted and were sold only to meet the same fate as Oscar. Chicks and baby bunnies were especially popular presents at Easter time, only to perish a few days later. In these enlightened times, the treatment of animals back then seems almost barbaric.